Angus and Dundee
40 Coast and Country Walks

The author and publisher have made every effort to ensure that the information in this publication is accurate, and accept no responsibility whatsoever for any loss, injury or inconvenience experienced by any person or persons whilst using this book.

published by
pocket mountains ltd
Jenny Wren, Holm Street, Moffat, DG10 9EB
pocketmountains.com

ISBN: 978-1-907025-15-0

Text and photography copyright © James Carron

The right of James Carron to be identified as the Author of this work has been asserted by him in accordance with the Copyright, Designs and Patents Act 1988

A catalogue record for this book is available from the British Library

Printed in Poland

Introduction

For walkers, Angus has it all – bracing coastal strolls, sheltered woodland walks, easy riverside rambles, airy moorland treks and stiff mountain ascents. The landscape and terrain is so varied, every day out can be different.

This guide contains 40 routes, the majority offering easy to moderate walks, with a few more challenging hikes to the summits of higher peaks. Together, they present a flavour of the immensely varied countryside, scenery and topography found here.

The county has a proud maritime heritage and there are 43km of coastline to explore. While an Angus coastal path remains in development, there are plenty of well-trodden seaside paths and clifftop trails linking spectacular beaches, striking geological features and secluded coves.

Inland, agriculture dominates the fertile plains of Strathmore, but amid the fields and furrows there are forests, rivers and lochs where low-level walks abound.

Head for the hills and you are spoilt for choice. The Angus Glens comprise of Glen Isla, Glen Clova, Glen Prosen, Glen Lethnot and Glen Esk, and the county includes part of the Cairngorms National Park. Each glen has its own distinct character. Isla is green, Clova craggy, Prosen peaceful, Lethnot wild and Esk remote. There are Munros – Scottish hills over 3000 feet high – to climb and long, winding valleys to explore.

The walks in this guide are divided into five sections. Four cover inland areas and

include the Angus Glens while the fifth explores the coastline. Each section begins with a summary of the area, offering a taste of what you can expect when you don your boots, plus a map to locate the start point of each of the routes.

Safety and what to take

The geographical make-up of Angus means that different weather conditions often prevail in different parts of the county, so be prepared for every eventuality, particularly on longer walks.

Sturdy walking shoes or boots are recommended for all routes. The majority follow good paths and tracks, but in some cases the terrain can be wet or muddy underfoot. Take wind- and waterproof clothing and ensure you have enough warm layers to enjoy the walk whatever the conditions.

Most of the walks in this book are suitable for families with children and, in some cases, can be completed by kids on bikes. Low-level routes that follow predominantly tracks and minor roads are usually suitable for all-terrain buggies.

The sketch map accompanying each route is intended to help plan the outing rather than as a navigational aid. The relevant Ordnance Survey Explorer or Landranger map should always be taken. On longer routes that cross open ground, a compass and the knowledge to use it is essential.

Some of the walks include sections along high and unfenced cliffs where special care should be taken, especially if you have children or a dog with you.

Access

Although the main towns and larger villages in Angus are well served by public transport, the remoter glens are less easy to reach without a car. While every effort has been made to include walks that can be reached by bus or train, this guide would be incomplete without routes in the glens. In some cases, the only form of public transport is the schoolbus, on term time weekdays, or demand responsive services that run on request and must be booked in advance. Timetables can be found at tourist information centres, from Traveline Scotland or on Angus Council's website (angus.gov.uk/transport) or, for Dundee buses, at dundeetravelinfo.com.

Responsible walking

The Angus countryside is a great resource for outdoor activities like walking. But that is only half the story. It also provides a living for a great many people, including farmers and foresters. To avoid conflict between walkers and those who work the land, it is important to enjoy the great outdoors responsibly.

Walkers in Scotland have long enjoyed the right to roam on just about any land with no requirements to stay on defined paths or rights of way. This position was ratified with the implementation of the Land Reform (Scotland) Act 2003 which gives everyone the right to be on most land, provided they act responsibly.

Always follow the Scottish Outdoor Access Code. Some of the walks in this guide cross land where farm animals graze or deer, mountain hare and groundnesting birds live. If you take a dog, it is important to keep it on the lead in such areas.

Occasionally you may encounter temporary access restrictions. This could, for example, be a forest track closed due to tree harvesting or a path shut because of erosion. Usually a diversion will be offered and if this is the case you should follow it. If there is no diversion, you may have to consult your map and work out an alternative route.

Wildlife

With its landscape of mountains, moors, lochs, woodland and coast, Angus offers a diverse natural habitat for a wide variety of animals, birds, insects and plants.

Improvements to water quality over recent years has seen an increase in bottlenose dolphins in both the Firth of Tay and North Sea while the shoreline and cliffs are home to seabirds like puffins, fulmars, shags and guillemots.

The county's many small lochs attract ducks, geese, swans and grebes and you may also spot osprey fishing. Other birds of prey such as buzzards, kestrels and sparrowhawks hunt over farmland and forestry while golden eagles and peregrine falcons dwell in the mountains.

Red squirrels, and roe and fallow deer, continue to thrive in the woodlands of Backmuir and Templeton. Montreathmont Forest, near Brechin, is a key destination for birdwatchers. The upland terrain of the Angus Glens, a mix of mountain, heather moor and forestry, is home to red and roe deer, otters, stoats, grouse and ptarmigan, while the higher slopes are carpeted in hardy mountain plants and alpine flowers.

The rivers of Angus attract birds like the kingfisher and at spots like the Rocks of Solitude on the River North Esk you can see salmon leaping as they head upstream to spawn in the autumn.

History
Angus lays claim to being the birthplace of Scotland, thanks to strong links with the Picts and its pivotal role in efforts to secure independence from the English in the early 14th century. During the Dark Ages, the Picts – a tribe of painted warriors – dominated Scotland. A Celtic people, they inhabited the lands north of the Firths of Forth and Clyde and divided the area into provinces. Angus formed part of the Circhenn heartland. The Picts successfully held off the invading Roman Army during the campaign of Emperor Severus in 210AD, but there were regular skirmishes with the Northumbrians, their neighbours in the south. During the 7th century, Lothian fell to Egfrith, King of Northumbria, but as Egfrith marched north through Strathmore, the Pictish king, Bridei, lured him towards Dunnichen Hill, near Forfar, trapping and killing most of them in a narrow cleft. It was a key victory for had they lost, historians believe Scotland may never have existed.

As Gaelic culture spread across Scotland,

the Picts died out. In 848AD, following the death of the last Pictish king, Drostan Mac Uuroid, the land of the Picts was united with the Kingdom of the Scots, creating the foundations of modern-day Scotland. They left behind an enduring legacy in the form of standing stones carved with pictures and mysterious symbols. These are to be found all over Angus – some of the best examples are at Aberlemno, Cossans, Eassie and Glamis.

Conflict with the English continued to occupy the Scots, most notably during the Wars of Independence in the 13th and 14th centuries. Following the sudden death of King Alexander III in 1286, the country was thrown into turmoil. John Balliol and Robert Bruce, grandfather of Robert the Bruce, both laid claim to the throne. The Guardians of Scotland turned to King Edward I of England to adjudicate, but he decided instead to invade. Numerous battles including at Bannockburn, where Robert the Bruce was victorious in 1314, followed. Although Bruce was now king of Scotland in the eyes of most Scots, his rule and Scotland's independence lacked recognition from England and the Pope. In a bid to rectify this, Bruce and Scotland's leading barons met at Arbroath Abbey in April 1320 to sign the famous Declaration of Arbroath, also known as the Declaration of Scottish Independence.

Despite this impassioned plea, it was not until 1328, when Bruce successfully invaded northern England, that his kingship and the nation's independence were at last recognised.

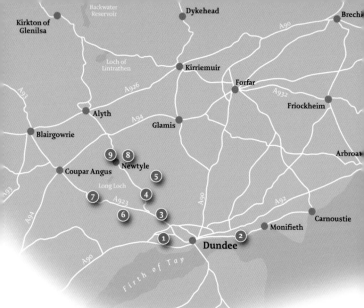

Scotland's fourth largest city, Dundee is a good base for exploring Angus. However, it also boasts many fine walks of its own, some urban, others rural. Dubbed the City of Discovery since the mid-1980s when Captain Scott's famous Antarctic expedition ship *RRS Discovery* returned to the place in which she was built, there is much to discover on foot. Two of the best-known local landmarks, Dundee Law, an extinct volcanic plug, and Balgay Hill, home to an observatory, offer easy hikes to elevated viewpoints. Waterfront rambles can be enjoyed along the estuary of the River Tay, Scotland's longest river, while Broughty Ferry, to the east of the city, and neighbouring Monifieth both offer fine seafront strolls.

The city's northern periphery is dotted with shady rural retreats like Camperdown Country Park, Templeton Woods and Backmuir Wood while the Sidlaw Hills, a range of low peaks stretching east from Perth into Angus, offer easy escape from the hustle and bustle of urban life amid a scenic backdrop of heather moor dotted with Scots pine trees.

Head west on either the Coupar Angus or Newtyle roads and the land is predominantly agricultural. But amid the fields and furrows, little peaks like Lundie Craigs and Kinpurney Hill speck the landscape while tranquil hidden lochs and leafy forests invite exploration.

Dundee, Auchterhouse and Newtyle

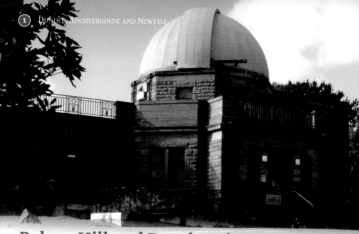

Balgay Hill and Dundee views

Distance 3km Time 1 hour 30
Terrain undulating surfaced tracks and
paths Map OS Explorer 380 Access bus
(22, 73) from Dundee city centre stops at
the end of Balgay Road

Rising above the houses and tenement
blocks in the west end of Dundee, Balgay
Hill is a pleasant leafy retreat from the
hustle and bustle of city life. It is criss-
crossed by a network of paths and tracks,
and perched on the 142m-high summit is
Mills Observatory.

Start the walk at the Eastern Gate
entrance to Victoria Park, located on
Balgay Road, opposite the top of Scott
Street. Originally called the Balgay Hill
Recreational Grounds, the park was
opened to the public in October 1871 by
the Earl of Dalhousie. There is plenty of
space to park here. Pass through stone
gateposts and round a barrier gate and

follow a wide surfaced track west. The way
hugs the heavily wooded base of Balgay
Hill and skirts above Victoria Park, a wide
swathe of grass dotted with trees.

The route runs level through an avenue
of trees to a junction where a track
branches right. Ignore this and carry
straight on, passing Royal Victoria
Hospital on the left to reach another
junction. The brick-built structure here
replaces a much older and grander
pavilion where generations of
Dundonians would pause during visits to
what was a cherished green space in a
heavily industrialised city.

Up ahead, the track leads into the city's
Western Necropolis. Bear right instead
and follow the track up through a rock
cutting. The way passes beneath Balgay
Bridge, an elevated wrought-iron walkway
linking Balgay Hill with the Western
Necropolis. Designed by George Hird, the

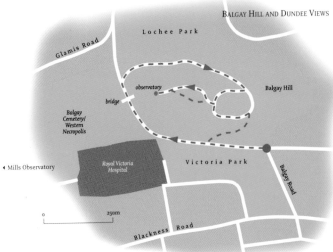

Lochee Park

Glamis Road

observatory

bridge

Balgay Hill

Balgay Cemetery/ Western Necropolis

◀ Mills Observatory

Royal Victoria Hospital

Victoria Park

Balgay Road

0   250m

Blackness Road

bridge, which has a 25m span, was erected in 1879. Vandalism forced its closure in 2002, but it re-opened six years later following an extensive renovation. Beyond the bridge, the track descends to a white barrier gate. Pass round this and, at the next junction, go right.

This track climbs gently round the northern flank of Balgay Hill, rising above the playing fields of Lochee Park. Views open out through mixed woodland to the Sidlaw Hills. Dundee Law is also visible, as is Cox's Stack, an 85m-high chimney constructed in 1866 as part of Camperdown Works, a vast jute mill.

Higher up, the track curves right. Just before it reaches its highest point, branch off on a path on the right that passes through a set of bollards. This rises steadily to a second set of bollards and another junction. Go right here and follow a track up to Mills Observatory.

This is the UK's only full-time public observatory. Beneath the 7m-high papier-mâché dome there is a 250mm Cooke refracting telescope. The classically-styled sandstone building also houses a small planetarium and display areas. The observatory is open throughout the year and admission is free.

To continue the walk, follow the track back down from the observatory to the junction immediately below and turn right. A pleasant path skirts round the slope below the building to rejoin the track to the east of the observatory. Carry straight on here, following a track lined with black lamp standards down the southern slope of Balgay Hill.

At the next junction, go right and the track curves down to the base of the hill. At the bottom, turn left and follow the track back to the start.

Broughty Ferry Beach

Distance 3.5km Time 2 hours
Terrain beach, level path, pavement
Map OS Explorer 380 Access Broughty
Ferry is well served by buses from Dundee

Bottlenose dolphins are becoming an
increasingly common sight in the Firth
of Tay and the best places to spot them
are from historic Broughty Castle and the
neighbouring beach, which regularly
wins accolades for the quality of its
bathing waters. This walk offers plenty of
scope for spotting these graceful marine
mammals: to stand the best chance of
success, visit on a summer evening.

The starting point for this walk is
Broughty Ferry Beach car park, just east of
the castle on The Esplanade. Descend
concrete steps to the beach, turn left and
walk east along the sand, passing a small
lifeguard station that is manned during
the summer months. It is not quite
Baywatch, but on a hot, sunny day the
beach draws swarms of bathers.

The crowds soon thin as you walk east.
Ahead Buddon Ness juts across the
horizon, marking the end of the firth and
the start of the North Sea, while across
the water Tentsmuir Forest bristles across
the skyline. When the tide is out the
mudflats attract birds like oystercatchers
and curlews, while the dunes up to the
left are a haven for sand martins.

Dolphin watchers should aim to visit
the beach when the tide is coming in as
the creatures tend to follow shoals of fish
upstream. They are also more likely to be
seen when the water is choppy.

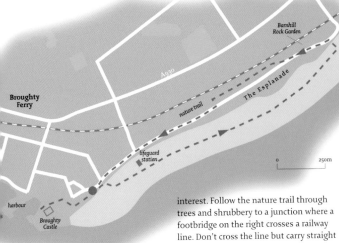

Further along the beach, the route negotiates a series of wooden groynes before passing round a headland. Continue along the sand until you reach a set of concrete steps at the top of the beach. Ascend these, cross the road and turn left, following the pavement past Barnhill Rock Garden.

Beautifully maintained by Dundee City Council and a band of dedicated enthusiasts, the garden – created on the site of a former golf course – covers two hectares and is open to the public throughout the year. Admission is free.

Adjacent to a large black sign welcoming visitors to the garden, a path leads into Broughty Ferry Local Nature Reserve. The reserve was created along the line of a former railway track, and information boards highlight points of interest. Follow the nature trail through trees and shrubbery to a junction where a footbridge on the right crosses a railway line. Don't cross the line but carry straight on, staying on the main path to reach another junction where there is a tunnel on the left. Again, go straight on, skirting between trees and bushes on the left and an area of open grassland to the right.

The path rises to a new apartment block. Go left and then right to meet The Esplanade. Cross, turn right and follow the pavement as it runs alongside sand dunes back to the beach car park.

Before heading home a visit to Broughty Castle is recommended. A couple of minutes' walk from the beach car park, admission is free and there are some great vistas over the firth from the viewing gallery on the top floor. Built in 1495, the stronghold has been altered and adapted over the years and, despite falling into ruin, it was rebuilt in the 19th century for military use.

◄ Broughty Ferry seafront

Templeton Woods

Distance 2km **Time** 1 hour
Terrain undulating woodland tracks and
paths **Map** OS Explorer 380 **Access** bus
(57, 59) from Dundee stops at the top of
Templeton Road, 500m from the car park

Despite such close proximity to Dundee,
Templeton Woods is a haven for wildlife.
Red squirrels and roe deer lurk in the
undergrowth while the leafy canopy is
home to buzzards, woodpeckers and
jays. Visit at dusk and there's a good
chance of spotting bats. A network of
paths and tracks make exploration easy
and there is a car park and visitor centre
just off the A923 Coupar Angus Road,
between Dundee and Birkhill.

From the east end of the car park, a path
curves right, crossing a footbridge to join a
forest track at an information board. Turn
left and walk east, following blue
waymarkers. The route passes through a
pleasant mixture of broadleaf and conifer
trees where you may see red squirrels
scampering through the undergrowth or
up and down the trunks in search of food.
This is one of the few places in the Dundee
area where they continue to thrive.

David Taylor, head forester to the 1st
Earl of Camperdown, planted Templeton
Woods in the early 19th century. Originally
much larger, they now cover 150 acres and,
although still a working forest, play an
important recreational role, attracting
walkers, cyclists and horseriders, as well
as wildlife enthusiasts.

The track rises steadily. Carry straight
on at the next junction encountered and
continue along the track until you reach
Gallow Hill watertower, concealed in the
trees to the left. At the junction below the
tower, turn right and descend quite

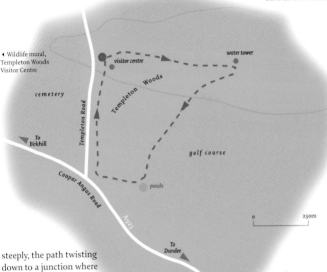

◄ Wildlife mural,
Templeton Woods
Visitor Centre

steeply, the path twisting
down to a junction where
there is a wooden footbridge on the left.

Go straight on and a long, unwavering
section of path leads to another junction,
where there are two wooden benches, a
great spot to rest and enjoy the
tranquillity of the woods. Again, continue
straight ahead and do likewise at another
junction just a few metres further on.

The path runs along the edge of
Downfield Golf Course to reach a pair of
wildlife ponds. Children will enjoy
exploring a rough trail that skirts around
the larger of the two pools.

The path meets a track at the ponds.
Turn left and follow this south. The track
curves right through tall beech trees
and, at the next junction encountered,
go right and head west until you reach a
wooden bridge spanning a drainage

ditch, close to Templeton Road.

Cross the bridge and take the path
heading north through the trees to meet a
forest track, just beyond another wooden
footbridge. Go left towards a metal barrier
gate and then turn right to follow a track
leading north through what used to be
the forest car park to Templeton Woods
Visitor Centre. Adorned with colourful
graffiti art depicting some of the birds
and plants found in the forest, the centre
is a great source of information on both
the forest and local activities organised by
the countryside ranger service.

If you fancy exploring further, a short
arts trail featuring a timber xylophone,
totem pole, Millennium Circle and a
variety of carved wooden benches starts
at the centre.

13

Dronley Wood

Distance 3km **Time** 1 hour 30
Terrain gently undulating path and track
Map OS Explorer 380 **Access** bus (57) from
Dundee stops at the Auchterhouse road
end, 2.5km from the start

Dronley Wood is a plantation of two
halves, split down the middle by a striding
line of electricity pylons. A modern-day
intrusion these metal monsters may be,
but rather than detract from the
enjoyment of the walk, they actually
enhance it, preserving a strip of moorland
habitat between the trees.

Forest Enterprise and the Auchterhouse
Community Woodland Action Group,
which looks after the network of paths,
manage 51-hectare Dronley Wood. A small
car park is provided for walkers, just off
the road linking North Dronley with
Kirkton of Auchterhouse.

Go through a metal pedestrian gate and,
to the left of the main forest track, pick up
a path that heads east through mature
beech trees and then stands of tall Scots
pine. The beeches are over 90 years old
and form a small enclave within the
plantation. The gradient is level and, for
the most part, the path is solid, although
there are a few muddy spots and, in
places, short detours have to be made to
avoid fallen trees. Although pine is
dominant, a good mix of ash, beech and
sycamore add diversity to the plantation.

The woodland feel is pleasantly airy, the
ground carpeted with bracken and
brambles. Look out for roe deer lurking in
the undergrowth and, to the left, enjoy
occasional glimpses through the trees to
the Sidlaw Hills.

In due course, the path emerges from
the trees into a wide grassy clearing

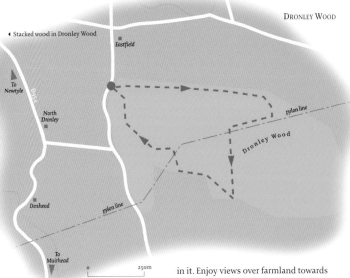

◄ Stacked wood in Dronley Wood

Eastfield

To Newtyle

North Dronley

pylon line

Dronley Wood

Denhead

pylon line

To Muirhead

0   250m

occupied by a pylon line and a separate line of overhead cables. To the left there is a fine view east over fields and farmland. Turn right at this point and follow a grassy path that heads west, running parallel with the high wires.

The route rises gently, crossing a patchwork of grass, heather and scrubland, dotted with scrubby trees and broom bushes. It is not uncommon to spot buzzards hunting here.

Pass a pylon on the left and, 25m beyond this point, turn left on an obvious path that leads south into the trees. The route weaves through Scots pines and, just beyond a clearing on the left, arrives at a track. Cross this and carry straight on.

The path reaches the southern edge of the forest at a wall with a pedestrian gate

in it. Enjoy views over farmland towards the villages of Muirhead and Birkhill before turning right to follow a trail along the boundary of the plantation. After a while, the way swings right, heading north along the edge of a field.

The path sticks close to the field boundary, a post and wire fence, for a way. However, when the fence makes a sharp left turn, the path continues straight on, rising gently to re-enter the clearing that divides Dronley Wood.

Passing below the pylon line, the path swings left before curving right further on. It passes below a line of overhead cables and leads back into the trees. The route runs flat through predominantly conifer trees before descending into a dip. As it climbs out, it curves right and then left ahead of the final descent down a bank of broadleaves to the car park.

15

Auchterhouse Hill

Distance 6km **Time** 3 hours
Terrain woodland paths, steep hill tracks;
navigation with an OS map and compass
is recommended **Map** OS Explorer 380
Access bus (138, 139) from Downfield,
Dundee, stops at Kirkton of Auchterhouse,
2km from the start

Carpeted in pink heather in summer and
peppered with gnarled old pine trees, the
upper slopes of Auchterhouse Hill are
bewitching, a fairytale landscape where
your imagination will run riot. There's
history too; a hill fort occupied this
prominent peak in turbulent times that
are a world away from the tranquillity that
greets walkers today.

Start in the Balkello Woodland car park,
on the minor road between Kirkton of
Auchterhouse and Tealing. Pass through a
metal gate leading into the woodland
and, from an information board and
pond, a wide grassy path curves left,

running along the top of grassland.

Ignore the first track you pass on the
right and, at the next junction, turn right
and continue to a Y-junction just within
the trees. Go left here and a steady incline
rises to another junction. Carry straight
on, passing through a gap in a wall and, at
a three-way junction a little further up,
take the middle path and follow it up to
the top of the plantation.

Covering 115 hectares, Balkello
Woodland was planted between 1993 and
1998 and incorporates an array of native
species, including Scots pine, birch, oak,
rowan, ash and alder.

Head for a wall at the top of the slope
and bear right, a grassy path leading
below an electricity pylon line to a stone
stile in an adjoining wall. Clamber over
the stile and join a track a few metres
further on. Once on the track, turn left
and walk west, the way running parallel
with a wall and the pylon line.

◄ Auchterhouse Hill

The route descends through bracken, passing a small pond, and travels below the pylon line once again to reach a junction. Turn right and the ascent of Auchterhouse Hill begins. The way rises through bracken and heather, passing under the pylon line and below quarry workings. There are various quarries dotted around the hills here; the last was worked in the 1960s.

Ignore various paths that come in from the left and right, and continue up the main track. The ascent is fairly strenuous, but in a while the way flattens out to reveal a wild plateau of grass and heather dotted with windswept pine trees.

The track curves right to reach a wooden gate and stile. Cross and descend to the next junction. Go right here and the way dips before earnestly tackling the northern slope of Auchterhouse Hill. It winds up through heather and old pines with heavy, drooping branches before flattening out

on the peak's eastern shoulder.

Where the route soon forks, go right and the path curves round the slope to meet a wider path just beyond a metal pedestrian gate. Turn right and follow it up to the summit, the site of an ancient hill fort and an excellent viewpoint with vistas south over the River Tay to Fife and east across neighbouring Craigowl Hill with its cluster of masts at the top.

Follow the same path back down, pass by the metal gate and carry straight on over the southern flank of Auchterhouse Hill. The way loops down to a junction below quarry workings. Turn left here and descend to another junction, where there is a metal gate. Go right and follow the track west to reach the stone stile leading into Balkello Woodland. Retrace your steps from here back to the car park.

Backmuir Wood

Distance 3km **Time** 1 hour 30
Terrain undulating woodland paths,
muddy in places **Map** OS Explorer 380
Access bus (57, 59) from Dundee stops in
Muirhead, 2km from the start

Backmuir Wood, to the south of
Muirhead, is a haven for wildlife and one
of the few places in Angus where red
squirrels thrive largely free from
disturbance by their destructive grey
cousins. Go quietly and you may also see
roe deer, the great spotted woodpecker,
jays and buzzards.

The walk begins at a Woodland Trust car
park at the southern tip of the 50-acre
plantation, on the minor road linking
Muirhead with Liff. Go through a wooden
gate at the right-hand end of the car park
(below a tall oak tree) and head north
along a grassy path flanked by bracken
and sheltered by mature oak trees.

A little way on the trail forks – take the
right-hand option and continue, passing a
path coming in from the left, to reach a
gate on the eastern edge of the
plantation. Cross a wider track here and
continue north, through stands of slender
silver birch trees. Ignore a couple of
narrow paths coming in from the left and
at the next major junction go straight on.

The path rises gently through mixed
woodland dotted with a few tall larches,
then crosses a small clearing carpeted in
bracken before heading back into the
trees to meet a gravel track, with a gate
leading out onto the road over to the
right. Turn left and, at the next fork, take
the path on the left.

Remain on the surfaced path, ignoring
paths branching to the left and right, and
continue alongside an area of tall Scots
pine trees where there is a good chance of
spotting red squirrels.

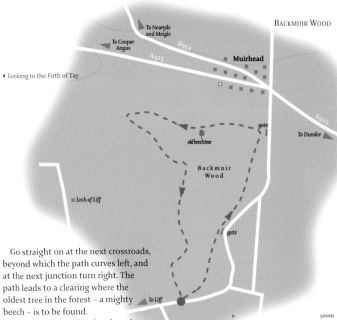

To Newtyle
and Meigle

To Coupar
Angus

B954

A923

◀ Looking to the Firth of Tay

Muirhead

A923

To Dundee

gate

old beech tree

B a c k m u i r
W o o d

gate

■ Loch of Liff

To Liff

0   500m

Go straight on at the next crossroads, beyond which the path curves left, and at the next junction turn right. The path leads to a clearing where the oldest tree in the forest – a mighty beech – is to be found.

Following the surfaced path to the right of the beech tree, go straight on at the next junction to make the winding journey through a delightful blend of mature trees and younger saplings where colourful jays may be seen. The path emerges at a bench on the edge of the plantation where you can enjoy fine views south over open fields to the Firth of Tay and the Lomond Hills across the water in Fife.

Turn left and the path runs parallel with the edge of the woodland, descending below tall Scots pines and curving left to reach a wooden bench and junction. Go right here and the path follows a post and wire fence before climbing briefly through

tall beech trees. This section of the walk can be muddy underfoot.

The route bears south, staying close to the edge of the plantation. At the next junction, ignore a grassy track on the left and carry straight on. Climb over a stony mound, then bear left, following a grassy path that can also sometimes be muddy. Continue to a seat carved in a fallen trunk and turn right, crossing stone slabs.

A grassy path leads from here through a plantation of younger trees, passing another tree trunk bench. Beyond a cluster of stones, the way reaches a gate leading into the car park.

Lundie Craigs and Ledcrieff Loch

Distance 7km **Time** 3 hours **Terrain** forest tracks, paths with well-graded ascents and descents; there are steep, unguarded drops below Lundie Craigs where extreme care is required **Map** OS Explorer 380 **Access** bus (59) from Dundee stops at Tullybaccart on request

Stocked with rainbow and brown trout, Ledcrieff Loch is popular with anglers, but walkers too will find themselves drawn to this spot by Lundie Craigs, an airy escarpment of volcanic rock that overshadows the peaceful tree-lined pool.

Start at Tullybaccart car park on the A923 Coupar Angus road. Cross the road and head along the track towards Tullybaccart Farm. Follow the track to the right of farm sheds and, behind the steading, the route curves left, rising gently through a metal gate.

Continue past a quarry on the right, following a sign for Ledcrieff Loch. The track passes TV aerials on a post and descends, curving right to enter Pitcur Wood. Ignore a grassy trail coming in from the left and stay with the main track as it swings right and begins a steady but well-graded ascent through the trees.

The way soon opens out, skirting above a field to the left. It swings left, passing below tall pine trees, and then right before straightening out for the final leg to Ledcrieff Loch.

Just before you reach the loch, go left on a track that descends through a metal gate below a grassy embankment at the west end of the water. The way curves left and rises through woodland, a mix of conifers, beech, oak and sycamore. It soon emerges from the trees at a viewpoint with vistas over Strathmore.

Stay on the track as it curves right for a long, steady ascent through a wide area of recently planted woodland, a mix of

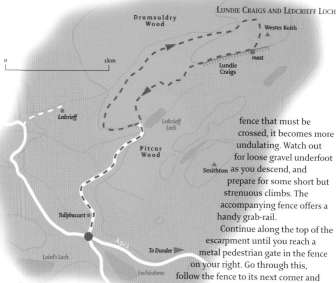

fence that must be crossed, it becomes more undulating. Watch out for loose gravel underfoot as you descend, and prepare for some short but strenuous climbs. The accompanying fence offers a handy grab-rail.

Continue along the top of the escarpment until you reach a metal pedestrian gate in the fence on your right. Go through this, follow the fence to its next corner and turn right on a grassy path that climbs briefly before levelling off. The path soon swings left. The route runs straight, crossing grassland over an area of recently felled woodland above the loch. Further on, it turns left, aiming for the trees at the far end of the clearing.

The path descends through woodland to the loch. If there are no anglers on the grassy embankment at the west end of the water, wander across it. If there are fishermen casting their lines, turn right at the bottom of the slope and walk a little further through the trees to meet the track followed earlier in the route. Turn left and follow the track below the embankment at the west end of the loch to the metal gate. At the junction above the gate, turn right to return to Tullybaccart.

species taking the place of the regimented lines of conifers that once grew here in Drumsuldry Wood.

Some 2km on from the viewpoint, the track swings left. Ignore a wooden gate on the right and continue to the next junction, a few metres on. Go right at this point and a track leads up to a metal gate and stile on the eastern boundary of the plantation. Cross the stile and follow the track up over heather moor to a mast on top of Lundie Craigs.

Pass through a wooden gate to the left of the mast compound and you begin the exhilarating hike along the top of the crags. Take great care – there is a long drop to your left. The elevated trail, which offers a bird's eye view of Ledcrieff Loch, runs level for a way, but beyond a wooden

◀ Lundie Craigs

Kinpurney Hill

Distance 5.5km **Time** 3 hours
Terrain road, path, open hillside with
steep climbs; navigation with an OS map
and compass is recommended; dogs
should be kept on a lead across sheep
grazing land **Map** OS Explorer 380 or 381
Access bus (57) from Dundee to Newtyle

Overlooking the Vale of Strathmore,
Kinpurney Tower is a prominent
landmark. Built on the summit of
Kinpurney Hill, near Newtyle, in 1774 by
landowner James McKenzie, it originally
housed an observatory. Now an empty
shell, it is the high point of this strenuous
yet rewarding hill walk.

Parking for this walk can be found on
Newtyle's North Street, adjacent to the
town's park. Leave the car park by its main
entrance, cross North Street and turn left,
following the pavement. Head out past

speed limit signs and continue along the
road, past the entrance to Burnmouth
Farm on the left. Follow the road over a
bridge and continue on the tarmac,
between agricultural fields, until Denend
Farm is reached.

Leave the road and turn right, passing
through the farmyard (the route is well
signed). Stay to the left of the farmhouse
and its outbuildings to reach concrete
steps rising to a wooden gate. Go through
this and follow a path into The Den, a
heavily wooded valley with a rich mix of
trees, including ash, elm, beech, rowan,
sycamore and a smattering of conifers.

The route follows the Denend Burn
upstream, passing a heavily silted
millpond. As you progress through this
delightful miniature gorge, there are some
little waterfalls and pools. The path is
good, with steps in places and, midway up,

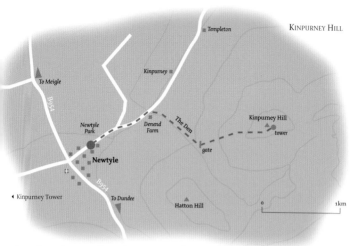

where the route passes through a pair of gates, there is a sturdy bench, ideal for a breather.

On reaching a wooden gate, the path finally exits The Den. From the other side of this, go left along a fence, crossing large stepping stones over a rather muddy burn to reach a waymarker. Go right, climbing up the grassy slope, aiming for a marker post visible further up the hill and from there continue to another.

The route heads up through a wide gap between gorse bushes, curving left as it continues to rise to another marker post. Beyond a reedy patch of ground, the route curves right and proceeds over a collapsed section of fence.

Next, the way passes a bench, where the tower looms into view above, and ascends a broad ridge to reach the remains of a gate. Beyond this there are a few windswept trees and then the tower itself.

When the observatory was abandoned, the tower fell into serious disrepair and in the early 1970s faced demolition. However, as it was such a well-known landmark, steps were taken to stabilise and preserve the structure. Empty and roofless, it affords little shelter in wet or windy conditions, but there is a superb vista from beneath its solid walls and a nearby viewpoint indicator installed in 2004 picks out the many points of interest.

There is also a trig point on the summit and in ancient times there was a hill fort and signal station here. Constructed during the Iron Age, the fort was oval in shape and was defended by a single rampart and ditch with an entrance on the west side of the hill. Investigations suggest the fort, which was discovered in the 1950s, was never completed.

To finish the walk, retrace your steps down the hill, continue through The Den to Denend Farm and return to Newtyle along the road.

Newtyle Railway

Distance 4.5km **Time** 2 hours
Terrain flat railway trackbed, minor road,
paths **Map** OS Explorer 380 or 381
Access bus (57) from Dundee to Newtyle

The Dundee to Newtyle Railway was one
of Scotland's earliest passenger lines,
opening in December 1831. Seven years
later the route was extended to Coupar
Angus and although both lines are now
long gone, the trackbed of the extension
has been preserved as a trail for walkers.

The path along the old railway line starts
at a car park adjacent to Newtyle Park, on
North Street. Head north on a solid gravel
path that runs between the park on the left
and open fields to the right. The way is
elevated above the surrounding land and,
as is to be expected from a railway walk,
runs level, making for easy walking.

Beyond the park, the route passes a
stone pit, formerly a railway turntable and
a junction where a second incarnation of
the Dundee to Newtyle Railway, which
closed to traffic in 1964, comes in from the
left. Both features are now largely
concealed by dense vegetation.

The first railway linking Dundee with
Newtyle and the fertile lands of
Strathmore incorporated a trio of inclines
up which the trains were hauled by fixed
steam engines. Initially, horses pulled
carriages and wagons over the level
sections, but in 1833 two steam
locomotives, the *Earl of Airlie* and *Lord
Wharncliffe*, entered service. In the 1860s
new tracks were laid, rendering the inclines
redundant and reducing the journey time.

Carry straight on and the line crosses a
bridge spanning a farm track and
continues to a bench constructed from old
sleepers. Here, the way skirts alongside a
low stone-built embankment and passes a
small set of steps, the start of a path

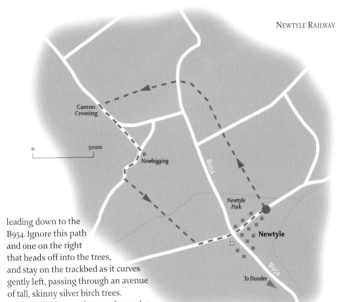

leading down to the
B954. Ignore this path
and one on the right
that heads off into the trees,
and stay on the trackbed as it curves
gently left, passing through an avenue
of tall, skinny silver birch trees.

A little further on the way descends to
meet the B954. Cross with care (visibility is
not good in either direction) and pick up a
track on the other side. Follow this along
the edge of a field and through a wooden
gate. A little further on, the track swings
left into another field. Rejoin the railway
trackbed here and walk west.

The route runs between two fields to
reach steps leading down to a minor road,
at Camno Crossing, midway between East
Camno and Newbigging. Once on the
tarmac, turn left, following a sign for Water
Backie. The road rises gently between
fields to a junction. Go right here, joining
a narrow lane that climbs to cottages.

At the centre of the cluster of cottages is
a junction. Turn right and follow the road
through Newbigging. Stay on the tarmac

as it curves left, leading to the start of a
path, on the left, signed for Water Backie.
Pass through a gate and follow the path
as it runs south between two fields.

As you progress, enjoy the views east
to Kinpurney Hill and its landmark tower.
At the top of the path, wooden steps rise
to another railway trackbed. Ignore these
and instead bear left and then right,
passing under an old railway bridge.
Follow the track ahead to meet the Coupar
Angus Road.

Turn left and let the Coupar Angus Road
lead you back into Newtyle. Cross Dundee
Road and carry straight on along North
Street, passing the village post office, to
reach the car park and the end of your
journey down memory line.

◄ Trackbed path

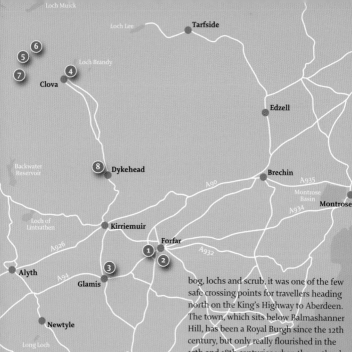

Forfar is the administrative hub of the county and gateway to the Angus Glens. A long-established market town with its roots firmly entwined in farming and weaving, its close proximity to the busy A90 makes for easy access. Indeed, Forfar has long been an important staging post and centuries ago, when the surrounding lands of Strathmore were a barren mire of bog, lochs and scrub, it was one of the few safe crossing points for travellers heading north on the King's Highway to Aberdeen. The town, which sits below Balmashanner Hill, has been a Royal Burgh since the 12th century, but only really flourished in the 17th and 18th centuries when the wetlands were drained and agriculture developed. Many visitors are drawn to the area by nearby Glamis Castle, childhood home of the late Queen Mother and, according to legend, Scotland's most haunted castle with a plethora of ghouls and ghosts. Those heading for Glen Clova, Glen Isla and Glen Prosen will find Forfar a good starting point with winding country roads leading from the town to all three. Clova is the most popular of the Angus glens, boasting a rich mix of forest, riverside and hill walks. More experienced walkers will find a clutch of Munros to tackle.

Airlie Monument ▸

Forfar, Glamis and Glen Clova

Forfar Loch

Distance 4km **Time** 2 hours
Terrain flat lochside paths and tracks
Map OS Explorer 389 **Access** Forfar is well
served by buses from Dundee and other
major towns in Angus

Forfar Loch Country Park boasts a rich
variety of wildlife. The gently rippling
water is home to wildfowl while
mammals including fox, otter and stoat
may be spotted in the parkland and trees
that hug the reedy shoreline.

Begin the walk at the Forfar Loch Ranger
Centre where there is free car parking and
a small visitor centre. Cross the car park
access road and follow a path signed
'Around Forfar Loch'. The route runs
between a caravan park on your left and a
children's play area on the right to reach
the east end of the loch where ducks and
swans congregate.

The way crosses parkland and passes, on
the left, a cricket ground and then rugby
pitches. The lochside is heavily overgrown
with reedy vegetation, plants and shrubs,
but along the way there are points where
you can get down to the shore and enjoy
views over the water.

Forfar Loch was originally much larger,
but over the centuries it has been
gradually reduced in size. The most
significant of these drainage operations
took place in the 18th century when the
Earl of Strathmore shrunk the loch by
1.5km in length and 5m in depth. Today, it
is 1.5km-long and up to 9m-deep.

Beyond the sports fields, the path leads
through a pleasant wooded corridor after
which it crosses an area of grass where the
route forks. Go right at this junction and
continue through woodland. The willow

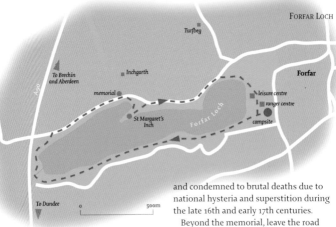

scrub here is managed by coppicing, which makes it a haven for wildlife.

Further on, the way crosses a wooden footbridge before continuing across open ground to the west end of the loch. Here, the path meets a track. Turn right and cross a metal bridge over the outflow. This is the start of the Dean Water, which flows west to Glamis Castle and eventually meets the River Isla. At the next junction, turn right to join a footpath that runs around the western tip of the loch.

As it approaches the north bank of Forfar Loch, the path crosses a wooden footbridge and rises to meet a gravel track. Join the track and walk east, passing a cottage, beyond which the walk continues along a surfaced road. As you go, look out for a small headstone on the left. Sheltered beneath a hawthorn tree and inscribed with the words 'The Forfar Witches, Just People', this simple tribute was placed as a memorial to women in the town who were branded as witches

and condemned to brutal deaths due to national hysteria and superstition during the late 16th and early 17th centuries.

Beyond the memorial, leave the road and go right on a gravel path that descends to a grassy picnic area and peninsula. Known as St Margaret's Inch, the narrow isthmus was once the site of a chapel founded by Queen Margaret, wife of the 11th-century king of Scotland, Malcolm Canmore. Historical evidence indicates that prior to the establishment of the chapel, the peninsula was, in fact, an artificial island. The chapel is long gone and today Forfar Sailing Club occupies this spot.

Rejoin the surfaced road and continue on it until a path (with a blue waymarker post) branches right, passing between metal bollards. Make the short detour to a viewpoint overlooking the loch before following the path to its next junction. Go right at this point and another path leads through bushes, emerging onto parkland at the eastern end of the water.

Head across the grass to join a surfaced path, turn right and follow this past a leisure centre to reach the ranger centre.

Balmashanner Hill

Distance 3.75km Time 2 hours
Terrain pavements and paths with some
steep climbs Map OS Explorer 389
Access Forfar is well served by buses from
Dundee and other major towns in Angus

Balmashanner Hill, known locally as
'Bummie', dominates the skyline above
Forfar. On the top, a tall sandstone tower
stands as a proud memorial to the local
men who died during the First World War.
Nearby, a viewpoint indicator picks out the
many points of interest that can be seen
from this elevated spot.

The walk starts at St James Road car
park in Forfar, where parking is free. Turn
left along St James Road to its junction
with Lour Road. Go left and follow Lour
Road, a quiet residential street. Head up
past Kirkriggs, on the right, and then turn
right into Hillside Road.

A short distance on, the road curves left
and runs fairly straight before curving left
again. At this point, go right through a
break in a high stone wall and a short
track leads into Reid Park, a large grassy
recreational area complete with
bandstand. Bear left on a path that leads
to a statue of former Forfar provost Peter
Reid, after whom the park is named.

Continue straight on and at the next
fork, bear left, following a path up
through rhododendron bushes. Climb
past an upper terrace with a cast iron
ornamental fountain and, at the top of
the park, bear right, following the path to
a gap in the wall and a sign for
Balmashanner Hill.

On the other side of the gap in the wall,
the path continues along the top of a field
of rough grassland where there are views
over Forfar. At the end of the field, the path

◄ Statue of Provost Reid

Forks; take the left-hand option.
A little way on, the path makes a
sharp left turn and climbs steeply
alongside a beech hedge.

At the top of the path there is a
T-junction. Go right here to reach
the tower. Designed by architect
Thomas R Soutar, built using local
sandstone and completed in 1921, it
carries the carved inscription:
'Erected in memory of the men of
Forfar and district who fell in the
great war, 1914-18'. Towering into the
sky and flanked by gnarled Scots pine
trees, it is a truly impressive sight.

Return to the T-junction and walk
straight on to reach a metal shelter
and viewpoint indicator gifted to the
town by local businessman James
Anderson in 1929. It highlights the
various hills and mountains that can
be seen from this spot on a clear day.

Descend north from the viewpoint,
the path following a fence and wall
into woodland. The route skirts
round the top of a quarry concealed
within the vegetation to your right before
dropping down through a wooded
corridor between fields to meet Lour
Road. Cross and go left on a path that
runs between trees and an open field
on the right.

Carry on along this path until you meet
a road at the end of a residential estate. At
this point, bear left up a tarmac path. It
climbs and curves right, passing children's

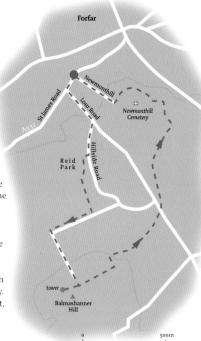

play equipment before running a narrow
course between gardens. At the end of the
path, carry straight on over a square and
follow Easterbank to its end, then turn left
to enter Newmonthill Cemetery.

Once in the cemetery, bear right and
follow the perimeter path round to the
exit leading out to Newmonthill. Follow
this street down to St James Road car park.

Ghosts of Glamis Castle

Distance **2km** Time **2 hours** Terrain **level paths, tracks; dogs should be kept on a lead** Map **OS Explorer 381** Access **bus (20C) from Dundee and (124, 125) from Forfar to Glamis Castle**

Stories of ghosts and ghouls abound at Glamis, said to be the most haunted castle in Scotland. A sealed chamber within the walls holds its own secrets while over the years numerous phantom sightings have been recorded in both the castle and its extensive grounds.

This walk starts in the car park at the rear of the castle and there is an admission charge to enter the grounds. Head north from The Pavilion Shop, adjacent to the car park, to join a grassy path signed as the River Dean Walk.

The way runs between fields occupied by the castle's herd of pedigree Highland cattle. As the path approaches the Dean Water, it swings right, running alongside the river, a gentle flow through leafy woodland and heavy foliage where you may spot otters, herons and kingfishers.

Continue to a stone bridge spanning the river, cross this and head straight up a surfaced track until you reach a red marker post. Turn right and a sheltered grassy path leads to the castle's walled garden. The first ornate gate you encounter is locked but go right and then left, following a red brick wall round to another gate, where there is a small exhibition detailing the history of the garden. Once the source of all the fresh produce consumed by the castle's inhabitants, it fell into disuse. Happily, however, it is currently being restored.

Descend south from the gate and cross Earl Michael Bridge to enter The Pinetum,

◄ Glamis Castle from the Italian Garden

a woodland of tall conifers established in 1870 and featuring a variety of species, most from North America. Look out for roe deer, red squirrels, stoats and woodpeckers as you proceed beneath the mighty trees.

At the southern tip of The Pinetum a bridge spans the Glamis Burn and the way curves left to reach the Princess Margaret Memorial. Turn right along a gravel path flanked by neatly trimmed hedges and then go left through a gate to enter the Italian Garden.

Established in 1910 by Lady Cecilia, wife of the 14th Earl of Strathmore and mother of the late Queen Mother, who was born at Glamis Castle, the Italian Garden features magnificent herbaceous borders, 17th-century-style summerhouses and gravel paths running beneath leafy canopies.

Make your way diagonally across the garden to a stone gazebo at the far right-hand corner and exit via the adjacent black metal gate. At the end of the next section of path, go right and the route emerges from woodland beyond a small pet cemetery.

Cross a track and go straight on along a path to the East Tower, an excellent point from which to take photographs of Glamis Castle. Established as a royal hunting lodge, the main keep dates from the 14th century when Robert the Bruce

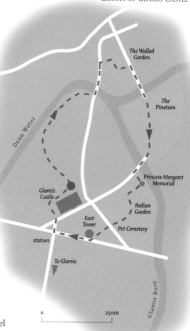

gifted the land to the Bowes-Lyons family. Much of the present structure, however, dates from the 17th century when the castle was extensively remodelled.

To conclude the walk, head west from the tower to meet the main drive by a pair of statues and then turn right. The route passes the castle's front entrance and skirts round the edge of the building to the car park.

The castle is open to the public throughout the year and guided tours last around an hour.

Loch Brandy

Distance 14.5km **Time** 5 hours
Terrain paths, steep in places and running
close to precipitous and unguarded drops
where great care should be taken;
navigation with an OS map and compass
is essential Map OS Explorer 388
Access limited bus service (801) from
Kirriemuir to Clova

The Clova Hotel has been offering
refreshment to weary travellers since the
1850s. Built on the once busy cattle drove
road linking Braemar with Angus, it
continues to revive visitors to the glen. It
is also the starting point for an upland
circuit to two corrie lochans, Loch Brandy
and Loch Wharral. Just over the old stone
bridge, on the single-track road to Glen
Doll, there is a small walkers' car park.

From the car park, cross back over the
bridge and head left, through the hotel
car park, passing a bunkhouse, to reach a
gate. Go through the gate and a path rises
into a sheltered copse of woodland,
emerging onto open moor higher up. It is
a stiff ascent, but the path is good and
height is quickly gained, offering superb
views over Glen Clova. There is more
climbing to contend with before the
gradient eases and the route strikes out
across heather that blooms bright pink in
the summer.

A final short pull reveals Loch Brandy, a
deep pool nestling in a rocky chasm
surrounded by high cliffs. It is a good spot
for a paddle or an invigorating wild swim,
but do take care; the water is deep and can
remain devilishly cold even on the hottest
summer day.

From the loch, bear left and follow the
steep path up onto The Snub, a shapely
shoulder separating Loch Brandy from
Corrie of Clova, and progress round the
top of the cliffs. The route runs above a

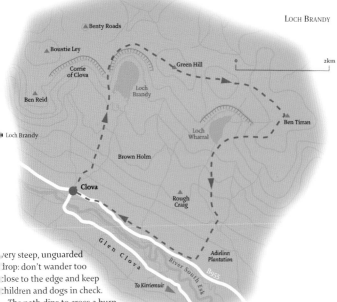

very steep, unguarded
drop: don't wander too
close to the edge and keep
children and dogs in check.

The path dips to cross a burn
before rising onto Green Hill. The
plateau is home to red deer and
mountain hare and you may also see
grouse, ptarmigan and, in summer, the
elusive dotterel.

Beyond Green Hill, the path splits.
Take the left fork and follow it for 1km,
then leave the security of the path and
strike out over open moor. Aim straight
for the obvious trig point on the summit
of Ben Tirran. Enjoy panoramic views
from the top of this hill before heading
south along the shoulder. Descend west
to pick up a path that drops towards
Loch Wharral. This is an equally dramatic
spot with a headwall of craggy cliffs
overshadowing the water.

From the southernmost point of the
lochan, a path descends to the top of
Adielinn Plantation and, from here, the
way runs down the west side of the trees.
Just before you reach the road at the
bottom of the slope, turn right on a path
that rises and falls over a series of glacial
moraines. This runs parallel with the road
to reach a fishing pond flanked by trees.
The path curves round the northern shore
to meet the B955 at a metal gate.

Join the road and follow it back to the
Clova Hotel for some well-earned
refreshment. Traffic is generally light and
there is a pavement for the majority of the
road walk.

35

White Water and Jock's Road

Distance **8.25km** Time **4 hours**
Terrain **undulating forest tracks, path**
Map **OS Explorer 388** Access **limited
bus service (801) from Kirriemuir to
Braedownie, 1km from the start**

This walk follows the frothing White
Water up into the wilder recesses of Glen
Doll before returning along a section of
Jock's Road, a well-trodden right of way
linking Braemar with Clova. Prior to
setting off, pop into the Glen Doll Ranger
Centre where there is a lot of useful
information on the local landscape, flora
and fauna and occasional exhibitions.

Leave the Forest Enterprise Glen Doll car
park by its main entrance. Pass a forest
walks sign and turn right, following a
track up to Acharn Farm. At the next
junction, by the farm, carry straight on,
following a sign for Braemar via Jock's
Road. The track descends through a gate

and passes below Glendoll Lodge,
formerly a youth hostel and now a private
house shrouded by woodland.

Continue to the next junction and go
straight on here, following signs for
Dounalt Walk. The wide forest road
follows the White Water upstream. Ignore
two tracks coming in from the right, one
just beyond Glendoll Lodge and the
second below the impressive crags of Craig
Mellon, and stay with the river. There are
many tempting glimpses of the water
through the trees and several clearings
where you can venture down to the bank
to rest by deep pools and admire
splashing waterfalls.

The route climbs to a junction where
Jock's Road bears right. Stay on the main
track and follow it as it dips to a clearing
where you can explore the riverbank and
view some more waterfalls.

A little further on, the track crosses the

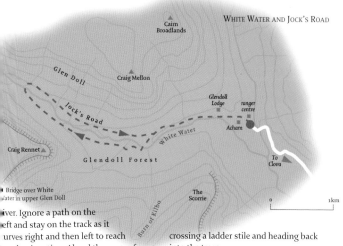

Caim
Broadlands

Glen Doll

Craig Mellon

Glendoll
Lodge

ranger
centre

Jock's Road

White Water

Acharn

Craig Rennet

Glendoll Forest

To
Clova

◀ Bridge over White
Water in upper Glen Doll

The
Scorrie

Burn of Kilbo

0   1km

river. Ignore a path on the left and stay on the track as it curves right and then left to reach another junction. Ahead the crags of Corrie Fee, a National Nature Reserve, rise above the tops of the trees. Go right here, crossing a bridge over a lively burn and enjoy an uninterrupted view of rocky Craig Mellon before continuing along the forest road. The way leads through a plantation of larch and Scots pine, and there are some massive boulders perched by the edge of the track.

The landscape ahead is much wilder and at the top of a long but well-graded incline the track ends and a path continues to the edge of the forest where a wooden footbridge spans the White Water. The terrain feels much more remote here, a vast amphitheatre encircled by high cliffs and great bluffs of rock. Cross the bridge and follow a narrow path alongside the forest fence to join Jock's Road. To the left, the route climbs steeply out of the glen, heading ultimately for Braemar via Tolmount. This walk, however, goes right,

crossing a ladder stile and heading back into the trees.

Jock's Road has a key place in Scottish rights of way history. In 1887 a group of shepherds who regularly drove their sheep over the rough mountain track joined forces with the Scottish Rights of Way Society to challenge a landowner who attempted to deny them access. After a lengthy and expensive court case, they were successful and established the route as a right of way, setting a precedent that has protected public access to scores of other routes through the Scottish hills.

The sheltered path undulates through pleasant woodland. Although dominated by conifers, rowan, ash and silver birch add interest and the way, carpeted in pine needles, is flanked by lush pillows of moss and ferns.

In due course, Jock's Road meets the main forest road at the junction encountered earlier in the route. Turn left here and follow the track back to the start.

Glen Doll and the River South Esk

Distance 3.5km **Time** 2 hours
Terrain gently undulating forest tracks,
path; dogs should be kept on a lead over
sheep grazing land **Map** OS Explorer 388
Access limited bus service (801) from
Kirriemuir to Braedownie, 1km from
the start

The River South Esk rises high in the
Angus hills at remote Loch Esk and flows
across the county to reach the North Sea
at Montrose. This short route joins it for
a tiny part of that lengthy journey,
savouring its youthful exuberance as it
skips through Glendoll Forest.

The walk begins at the Forest Enterprise
Glen Doll car park adjacent to the Glen
Doll Ranger Centre. Head towards the exit
at the east end of the car park and,
following a sign for South Esk Walk, take
the path out to join the access road. On
the tarmac, turn left and cross a bridge
over the River South Esk. On the other
side, bear left through a gate where a
good track sets off up the glen.

Initially the route crosses open
grassland dotted with trees where sheep
graze. You may also spot red deer here
and it is not unusual to hear the
unmistakable call of cuckoos in the trees
across the river, above Glendoll Lodge.

The route follows the River South Esk
closely for the first 1km of the walk, but
then veers away, a gentle incline rising
past a large patch of recently felled
forestry on the right. Flanked by trees on
the left, the track reaches a bridge
spanning the Cald Burn. Thanks to felling
it is now possible to see some impressive
waterfalls further upstream.

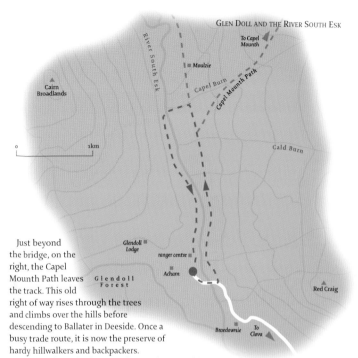

GLEN DOLL AND THE RIVER SOUTH ESK

River South Esk

To Capel
Mounth

Moulzie

Capel Burn

Capel Mounth Path

Cairn
Broadlands

Cald Burn

0   1km

Glendoll
Lodge

ranger centre

Acham

Glendoll
Forest

Red Craig

Braedownie   To
Clova

Just beyond the bridge, on the right, the Capel Mounth Path leaves the track. This old right of way rises through the trees and climbs over the hills before descending to Ballater in Deeside. Once a busy trade route, it is now the preserve of hardy hillwalkers and backpackers.

Carry on along the forest road to reach a high metal gate. Don't go through this but turn left, following a path through trees and over open ground to a wooden footbridge spanning the river. From here, there are views north up the glen towards Broom Hill and Moulnie Craig and there is a well-placed wooden bench if you fancy taking the weight off your feet for a minute or two.

Cross the bridge and follow the path downstream. Sheltered by tall, densely packed conifers and carpeted with pine needles, it is a very pleasant riverside

ramble. A little way down the valley, the water passes through a more tranquil section, the slow flow meandering through the trees before descending over the rocky riverbed with more vigour. Designated a Special Area of Conservation, the river boasts Scotland's largest population of freshwater mussels.

The path gently rises and falls and, as it nears its end, climbs away from the river to meet a fence on the right. Follow the fence to emerge from the trees at a grassy field dotted with picnic benches. Just beyond this point the car park is reached.

◀ River South Esk

Driesh by the Kilbo Path

Distance 10.5km **Time** 4 hours **Terrain** a strenuous ascent of a Munro on forest tracks and hill paths; navigation with an OS map and compass is essential; dogs should be kept on a lead across sheep grazing land **Map** OS Explorer 388 **Access** limited bus service (801) from Kirriemuir to Braedownie, 1km from the start

If you are looking to tackle your first Munro, where better to start than Driesh? Generations of hillwalkers have cut their Munro-bagging teeth on this fine peak which is very accessible, thanks to the Kilbo Path, a long-established right of way linking Glen Clova with Kilbo in Glen Prosen. Although strenuous, the ascent is well graded and, on a clear day, the views from the top are outstanding.

The hike begins at the Forest Enterprise car park adjacent to the Glen Doll Ranger Centre. Exit the car park by its main entrance, passing a forest walks sign, and turn right, following a track up to Acharn Farm. At the next junction, by the farm, carry straight on, following a sign for Glen Prosen via the Kilbo Path. The track descends through a gate and passes below Glendoll Lodge.

Continue to the next junction and turn left, following a sign for Doll Walk. A little further on, there is a Kilbo Path marker post. Beyond this, the track crosses a concrete bridge over the White Water.

At the next junction, stay on the main track, ignoring grassy paths that branch left and right. It curves right and a steady incline prompts legs and lungs into action. Further up, beyond a hairpin bend, the Kilbo Path (signed) branches right

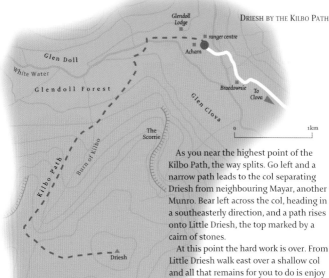

As you near the highest point of the Kilbo Path, the way splits. Go left and a narrow path leads to the col separating Driesh from neighbouring Mayar, another Munro. Bear left across the col, heading in a southeasterly direction, and a path rises onto Little Driesh, the top marked by a cairn of stones.

At this point the hard work is over. From Little Driesh walk east over a shallow col and all that remains for you to do is enjoy an airy and undemanding ascent to the top of Driesh. On the summit, which is 947m above sea level, there is a trig point nestling in a circle of stones that provides shelter from the elements for a well-earned rest and snack.

There are views aplenty to savour. Mayar lies to the west while Broad Cairn and Lochnagar dominate the vista to the north. To the south, the hills are lower but no less dramatic and you should be able to identify the outline of Backwater Reservoir.

To complete the walk, retrace your steps over Little Driesh to the col and rejoin the Kilbo Path for the descent to Glen Doll.

For a longer day in the hills, many Munrobaggers combine their ascent of Driesh with a hike over Mayar, descending back into Glen Doll via Corrie Fee.

and rises into the forest, accompanied by a small burn. The ascent is now more arduous, but there is brief respite further up when you emerge from the trees onto a track.

Cross the track to continue by the path over open hillside. Higher up, the way is once again consumed by trees, but the top of the plantation is not far off. The path crosses the lively Burn of Kilbo by stepping stones and climbs through a gate to emerge from the forest.

The Kilbo Path rises from here over the Shank of Drumfollow. It is a long but well-graded climb and, as height is gained, vistas open out over Glendoll Forest to the hills and mountains beyond.

Airlie Monument and The Goal

Distance 7.5km **Time** 4 hours
Terrain steep climbs on forest track,
moorland path, minor road; navigation
with an OS map and compass is essential;
dogs should be kept on a lead across
sheep grazing land **Maps** OS Explorer 381
and 388 **Access** limited bus service (121,
13, 220, 801) stops at Dykehead, 2km from
the start

Airlie Monument is a prominent
landmark, visible from miles around.
Erected in 1901 in memory of the 9th
Earl of Airlie, it marks the start of an
exhilarating ridge walk crossing the
high ground between Glen Clova and
Glen Prosen.

The walk begins at a small woodland car
park 2km west of Dykehead on the narrow
Glen Prosen road. Leave the car park and
head up a track that rises through tall
pine trees. Signed with occasional
waymarkers, the track curves left and then

right. The ascent is quite strenuous, but
further up the slope the gradient eases as
the way contours round the hillside to
reach a junction.

Go left at this point and prepare for
some more climbing, the route rising
steadily through the trees before
eventually emerging from the forest just
below the Airlie Monument. The red
sandstone tower is 30m-high and cost
£1300 to build. It commemorates the life
of David William Stanley Ogilvy, the 9th
Earl of Airlie, who died in battle while
gallantly leading his regiment, the 12th
Lancers, at Diamond Hill, near Pretoria,
during the Boer War.

The tower is an impressive structure
when viewed from below, with some
interesting carved panels set into the
stonework, but unfortunately there is no
access to the interior.

From the tower, a grassy track strikes
north over Tulloch Hill. It runs level

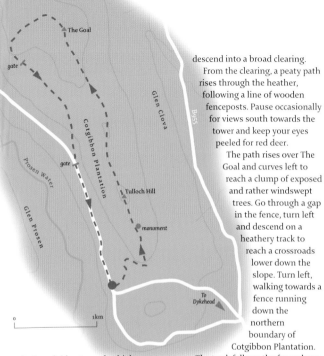

descend into a broad clearing. From the clearing, a peaty path rises through the heather, following a line of wooden fenceposts. Pause occasionally for views south towards the tower and keep your eyes peeled for red deer.

The path rises over The Goal and curves left to reach a clump of exposed and rather windswept trees. Go through a gap in the fence, turn left and descend on a heathery track to reach a crossroads lower down the slope. Turn left, walking towards a fence running down the northern boundary of Cotgibbon Plantation. The track follows the fence down to a high metal gate.

Go through the gate and a good track leads through the forest, crossing a number of felled patches. The way descends to a metal gate and, beyond this, meets the Glen Prosen road. Turn left and follow the road, normally very quiet, back to the car park. Flanked by woodland on the left, it runs above grassy fields grazed by sheep, cows and an army of rabbits.

across the broad ridge to reach a high wooden gate and ladder stile. Cross the stile and continue north, enjoying views over Glen Clova to the right and Glen Prosen to the left.

The way dips, crossing reedy, mossy and grassy ground before rising to a wooden gate at the edge of woodland. Go through the gate and follow a grassy corridor through the trees to reach another gate and ladder stile. Cross the stile and

◂ Descending to Cotgibbon Plantation

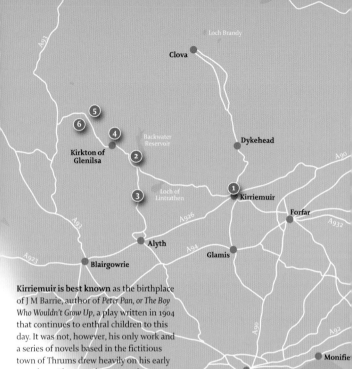

Kirriemuir is best known as the birthplace of J M Barrie, author of *Peter Pan, or The Boy Who Wouldn't Grow Up*, a play written in 1904 that continues to enthral children to this day. It was not, however, his only work and a series of novels based in the fictitious town of Thrums drew heavily on his early years here. The son of a weaver, the cottage where he was born is now a museum run by the National Trust for Scotland and when he died he was laid to rest in the local cemetery.

Kirrie, as the town is known locally, is a fascinating place to explore on foot, a chaotic maze of claustrophobic closes, narrow lanes and twisting alleys revealing quaint little shops and unexpected architectural gems. It is not, however, an easy place to negotiate in a car, something you will need if you wish to explore the

delights of nearby Glen Isla fully.

Head out of town on the B951 and great walking country abounds. A trio of artificial lochs – Backwater Reservoir, Loch Shandra and Auchintaple Loch – lurk beneath heavily wooded slopes while the prominent summit of Mount Blair offers unparalleled views over the remote upper reaches of Glen Isla, also known as the Green Glen, where much higher mountains dominate the landscape.

Peter Pan Statue in Kirriemuir ▸

Kirriemuir and Glen Isla

Kirrie Hill and Barrie's Birthplace

Distance 3km **Time** 2 hours
Terrain modest ascent on pavements, tracks, paths **Map** OS Explorer 381
Access bus (20, 22) from Dundee and (20, 25) from Forfar to Kirriemuir

Born and raised in Kirriemuir, J M Barrie, creator of *Peter Pan*, was also buried here upon his death in 1937, his family turning down the offer of a ceremony at Westminster Abbey in London. This walk visits both his birthplace and the cemetery where he was laid to rest.

Start at Kirriemuir's Reform Street car park, where parking is free and there are public toilets. Leave the car park by its main entrance, turn left and walk along Reform Street, passing a police station and post office. Cross and turn right into Roods. Head up past the Co-operative Supermarket and continue until you reach a school patrol sign near the top of the hill.

Turn right into a lane, signed 'Public footpath to Camera Obscura', and follow the route up between houses and alongside a stone wall bordering a quarry down to your right. The track rises above open fields, offering views over Kirriemuir and the fertile plains of Strathmore.

The track soon enters parkland and over to the left is Barrie Cricket Pavilion. This small building houses Kirrie's Camera Obscura, run by the National Trust for Scotland and Angus Council. Open from April to September, it is one of only three camera obscuras in Scotland.

To the right is Hill Cemetery, entered via a pedestrian gate with a prominent sign for Barrie's grave. Once in the cemetery, turn right and follow a surfaced path down to reach a small set of steps on the left. At the top a gravel path leads to the author's final resting place.

Carry on along the gravel path and turn

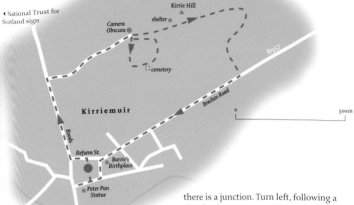

left, climbing steps with a metal handrail. Continue up to the main cemetery gates (normally locked) and go left, passing the town's war memorial, to reach the pedestrian gate.

Outside the cemetery, turn right and follow a track alongside the cemetery wall, signed for 'viewpoint'. Further on, ignore a path on the right signed for the town centre and continue past the James Wilkie of Appin Memorial Shelter, erected in 1928.

At the next junction, where there is an ancient standing stone, go right and walk to a covered reservoir. Bear left and head round the north side of the reservoir, enjoying views over farmland towards the Angus Glens.

As the path descends through mixed woodland, it curves to the right and passes below a former quarry now popular with rock climbers. Below this,

there is a junction. Turn left, following a sign for the town centre.

Where the path meets Brechin Road, turn right and head along the pavement into town. As you near the junction with Reform Street and School Wynd, keep an eye open for Barrie's Birthplace on the left. The neat, whitewashed cottage is now in the care of the National Trust for Scotland. Open from April to September, the museum houses manuscripts, diaries and photographs that belonged to Barrie.

Beyond the cottage, go left into School Wynd and then right into Bank Street. Walk along this narrow street of shops to a square where there is a bronze statue of Peter Pan standing outside the former townhouse, the oldest building in Kirriemuir and now home to a museum and tourist information centre.

To complete the walk, head back along Bank Street and duck through Manse Close (next to Bertram's Butcher) to reach Reform Street car park.

Backwater Reservoir

Distance 12km Time 4 hours
Terrain undulating track, path, minor
road; dogs should be kept on a lead across
sheep grazing land Maps OS Explorer 381
and 388 Access limited bus service (800)
from Kirriemuir stops at the end of the
Backwater Reservoir access road, 1.5km
from the start

Opened by the Queen in 1969, Backwater
Reservoir is 3km long and, together with
nearby Loch of Lintrathen, supplies water
to almost 300,000 people in Dundee,
Angus and parts of Perthshire. This route
combines tracks, paths and a minor road
to offer a pleasant low-level circuit.

Start at the public car park at the west
end of the Backwater Dam, which is 1.5km
north of the B951 Glen Isla road. Cross the
road, pass between stone gateposts and
head north on a surfaced track that hugs
the west shore of the reservoir. It passes

below a house and leads briefly through
woodland before running across open
ground that offers views across the water
and north up Glen Damff.

Although the project to build Backwater
Dam was initiated by Dundee Corporation
in 1964, it was completed by the newly
created East of Scotland Water Board in
1969 and is now operated by Scottish
Water. The dam was the first in Britain to
use chemical grouting to create a
waterproof barrier below the embankment.

With a solid track underfoot, the walking
is undemanding and good progress is
easily made. The next significant landmark
is a waterside chalet, down to the right.
Beyond this, the track is engulfed by
woodland once again.

The trees are but a brief interlude and,
beyond a gate, the track leads across an
open field. At the far end of the field, the
track curves right and then left, rising

towards forestry. Continue on the track until you reach a junction, then branch right on a path signed for Glen Damff. This enters a plantation of pine and larch, scattered with pine needles and rotting fallen branches, and leads through the trees to a gate at the other side of the woodland.

Go through this to descend by a rutted track running alongside a crumbling stone wall. This crosses grazing land where sheep share the grassy pickings with hare. There are a couple of gates to negotiate on the way down before you reach a wooden bridge spanning the Glendamff Burn at the bottom of the slope. The ground immediately before the bridge can be boggy.

Cross the bridge and head up to a gate in a wall. On the other side there is a track. Join this, turn right and the route leads past an empty cottage at Barny. Continue along the track and, beyond two sets of metal gates, head through a farmyard and skirt the southern flank of Cuilt Hill to reach Glenhead Farm.

The track descends to a junction where it meets the public road. Turn right and continue down past a farm shed on the left to cross the Hole Burn. The return leg along the eastern side of the reservoir begins here and follows a minor road for its entirety.

There is little traffic and, aside from a couple of plantations, the road passes through pleasant open country with no shortage of views over the reservoir and surrounding countryside.

At the southern end of the reservoir, the road swings right to cross the Backwater Dam, an 800m-long embankment that holds back 25 million cubic metres of water. To your left, a grass slope descends to associated buildings and the Back Water, which runs into Loch of Lintrathen, 5km south of Backwater Reservoir in Glen Isla.

Reekie Linn

Distance 500m **Time** 1 hour
Terrain gentle ascent on a good path, but take great care as it runs along the top of unguarded 45m-high cliffs
Map OS Explorer 381 **Access** demand responsive bus service (122) from Blairgowrie via Alyth to Bridge of Craigisla

The Victorians first put Reekie Linn on the tourist map and it has remained a firm favourite with visitors to Angus. The county's most spectacular waterfall, it drops more than 20m through a deep tree-lined canyon, throwing up a great mist of water. Seek it out, but take care: there are perilously steep drops along the way.

Reekie Linn is located just off the B954, 6km north of Alyth. There is a small car park with a pleasant riverside picnic area at Bridge of Craigisla where this short walk begins.

Head for a gate at the east end of the car park, where there is a board with information on the falls, the geology of the area and some of the wildlife that may be seen. Go through the gate and follow a delightful riverside path through a narrow corridor of mixed woodland separating the river on the right from open fields on the left.

The path runs flat for a time before rising gently. It is possible to scramble down a sloping section of the bank to a rocky promontory at the top of the waterfall, but you need to be careful if you plan to venture off the path. Although the slope itself presents no real danger, the rocky outcrop sits directly above the waterfall and a slip here could end in disaster.

Better to stay with the path as it leads safely round the top of an unprotected 45m cliff, which plunges straight down

◄ Reekie Linn

into the river, to a viewpoint beneath an old oak tree from where the falls are revealed in all their glory.

In normal conditions, the River Isla drops first over a 6m-high upper fall before cascading down an 18m-high lower section into a deep, black, frothy pool at the base of the gorge. When the river is in spate, these two falls combine with dramatic effect. The falls throw up great clouds of spray and it is from this that they got their name. The word *reekie* means 'smoke' or 'mist' while *linn* is Gaelic for 'deep or dark pool'. The pool beneath the falls is more than 30m deep.

At the base of the waterfall, there is a dark cave called Black Dub where, according to local folklore, an outlaw hid out until one night the devil appeared before him in the form of a huge black dog. Judging that a quiet cell was a better option, he turned himself in to the authorities the following day.

From the viewpoint, follow the path back to the car park and, if the weather is good, while away time in the riverside picnic area below Bridge of Craigisla.

If you are feeling particularly adventurous, a less walked path runs along the south side of the Reekie Linn gorge. Cross Bridge of Craigisla and follow the road up past a telephone box until you reach a squat stone gatepost on the left. Go through the gap in the wall, cross a bridge made from two railway sleepers and turn left a few metres on.

Beyond a sign warning of the dangers of steep cliffs, the path splits. The left-hand arm descends to a viewpoint overlooking the falls while the path on the right runs above the river for some distance and offers a very pleasant woodland wander; again, take care as there are steep, unguarded drops in many places.

Loch Shandra

Distance 8.5km **Time** 3 hours
Terrain steep climbs on forest road, paths, hill tracks, may be boggy; navigation with an OS map and compass is essential; dogs should be kept on a lead across cattle grazing land **Maps** OS Explorer 381 and 388 **Access** limited bus service (800) from Kirriemuir stops in Kirkton of Glenisla, 1km from the start

Although artificial, Loch Shandra blends perfectly with the surrounding landscape of rolling hills, moorland and forestry. This walk visits the loch before rising past two derelict farms onto wilder hillside and incorporates part of the long-distance Cateran Trail walking route.

Start at Forest Enterprise's Glen Isla car park at Freuchies, 1km east of Kirkton of Glenisla. On the north side of the car park,

go left and follow a forest road signed for 'Glen Prosen and Glen Clova by Kilbo Path'. The route rises gently through a plantation of pine and larch trees, running parallel with a burn down to your left.

In due course, the track flattens off and, as it nears Loch Shandra, there are tempting glimpses of the water through the trees. Continue on the track until you reach a wooden gate on the left; go through this and then another gate a few metres further on.

The route crosses a wooden bridge spanning the outflow of the loch and strikes across the embankment at the southern end. The loch is popular with anglers fly fishing for brown trout. Aim for a corrugated iron boathouse at the far end of the embankment, savouring views north over the water towards Badandun Hill.

Behind the boathouse, adjacent to a picnic table, the embankment path meets a track. Turn right and follow this along the west side of the loch. As you approach the north end of Loch Shandra, where small pockets of woodland hug the shoreline, look out for heron, swans and wildfowl in the reeds.

Leaving the loch behind, the track fords a tiny burn and arrives at a junction with a Cateran Trail marker post. Go straight ahead, the track rising quite steeply to a metal gate. Don't go through the gate, but instead go right, descending a grassy slope to another gate a few metres below. Go through this gate and follow a rough track across a burn; it can be wet and muddy underfoot.

From here, a grassy track takes you up over a field where cattle usually graze. Over to your right are the ruins of Craignity, an abandoned farm, while to the left there is a great view of Mount Blair. At the top of the field, the track passes through a metal gate and continues across a second field. As it approaches a wall and fence, it swings right and rises to a pair of wooden gates at the top left-hand corner of the field. Go through the right-hand gate onto a track which leads to a derelict farm cottage at Craighead.

Follow the track through the farmyard and, at the far end, swing right and climb to a high gate above a wooden shed. Go through the gate and walk straight on. The track leaves the shelter of tall pine trees and crosses open moor, descending through a long sweeping left-hand bend before rising to a gate.

On the other side of the gate, at a Cateran Trail marker post, go left and follow a grassy path which descends a heathery slope to a gate and stile. From here, the path carries on down to the base of the valley where you cross a burn before heading over moorland. Cateran Trail waymarkers lead you back to Loch Shandra and its boathouse. Retrace your steps to the car park via the forest road.

◄ Boathouse on Loch Shandra

Auchintaple Loch

Distance 5km **Time** 2 hours
Terrain steep climbs on forest and
moorland tracks, path **Map** OS Explorer 388
Access demand responsive bus service
(122) from Blairgowrie stops at Meikle
Forter, 1km from the start

Auchintaple Loch is a real hidden gem. It
has long been a favourite with anglers,
but few walkers ventured this way until
the arrival of the Cateran Trail. The long-
distance path forms part of this circuit
that crosses open moor and hillside
before descending to the sheltered stretch
of water and quaint boathouse.

This walk starts in Glen Isla just south of
the bridge over the River Isla at Little Forter.
A small layby can accommodate a couple of
cars here. (Alternative parking is available at
Folda, 600m south of the start on the road
to Kirkton of Glenisla.) Following a sign for
Auchintaple Loch, cross a ladder stile and

head up a good track. It is quite a strenuous
pull, but there are views back over Mount
Blair and Forter Castle should you need an
excuse to pause from time to time.

The route rises to a junction where the
main track sweeps right. Leave it here and
carry straight on, following a Cateran Trail
waymarker. An excellent hill track climbs
towards Badandun Hill, crossing a stile by
a wooden gate a little further up the slope.

Continue to a wide grassy junction and
bear right, following another Cateran Trail
marker. The track curves right, crossing a
small burn and then swings left after
passing between two metal gateposts.

Here you catch your first glimpse of
Auchintaple Loch, down to your right, with
Mount Blair in the background. It is an
artificial loch, created in 1884 for fishing
and, with trout the main catch, continues
to prove popular with anglers today.

After a climb, the route reaches its

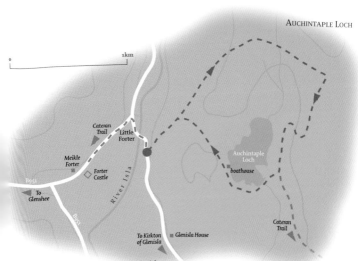

highest point, a junction above a ladder stile spanning a stone wall. Pause to admire the landscape, then turn right, the track descending towards a forestry plantation. Just before the trees are reached, look out for a wooden Cateran Trail waymarker, on the right, into which are carved a trio of bearded faces.

The Cateran Trail is a 103km-long circular route that starts and finishes in Blairgowrie and weaves its way through the countryside of Perthshire and Angus. It is named after the Caterans, marauding cattle thieves who plundered farms in the Highlands from the Middle Ages through to the 17th century.

Cross a stile and enjoy a pleasant, sheltered walk through the trees. Stay on the main track as it loops down to reach a gate and stile. Don't cross this stile, but instead bear right on a narrow path running through the heather. It descends

to cross the loch outflow. When the water is low, the crossing is easy. If the water is high, aim for a panel of wood and wire fencing where rocks assist.

On the other side of the outflow, a wooded promontory is worth exploring before returning to the path. This then crosses an embankment at the southern end of the loch and follows the heathery shoreline to a high gate. Go through this gate, entering woodland, and then pass through another gate a little further on to reach a two-storey stone boathouse perched by the edge of the water.

The track meets a junction behind the boathouse. Go straight on and, in a short distance, it leaves the trees at a gate. Ignore a track coming in from the right and continue straight ahead. The way drops down to the junction encountered earlier in the walk. Go left and descend to the road.

◀ Boathouse on Auchintaple Loch

55

Mount Blair

Distance 6km **Time** 3 hours
Terrain strenuous ascent on narrow hill
paths, returning by track and minor road;
boggy in places; navigation with an OS
map and compass is essential; dogs
should be kept on a lead across sheep
grazing land **Map** OS Explorer 387
Access demand responsive bus service
(122) from Blairgowrie stops at Meikle
Forter, 2km from the start

Mount Blair may be a low hill, but it is
one of the best viewpoints in Angus and,
on a clear day, it is possible to see a
panorama of peaks from the top.

The most direct route up is to follow a
track rising over the northern slope from
the B951 near Cray. It is, however, a rather
uninspiring slog. This route comes in
from the east with a more scenic
approach, but it is a very strenuous climb
and some sections of the path are
indistinct, requiring good route-finding.

Start at a large roadside layby just north
of the cottage at Altaltan on the B951 in
Glen Isla. Cross a stile to the left of a pair
of metal gates and, ignoring a track to the
right, head over an area of flat grass
between trees. Ascend the grassy slope
beyond and aim for a lone tree. About 20m
up from this tree, bear left on a stony,
grassy path that rises onto a shoulder.

Once on the shoulder, head right and
follow an indistinct grassy trail that
meets a more obvious path higher up.
This rises north between two lone trees –
the higher of the pair clings to a rocky
crag. Pass below this tree and carry on
along the path.

Further on, it peters out. Bear left up the
slope to join another narrow trail that
leads north to a small rocky outcrop.

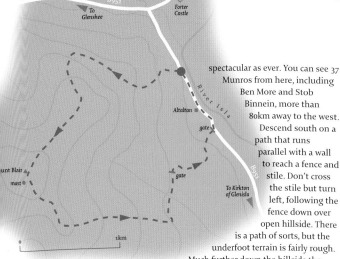

spectacular as ever. You can see 37 Munros from here, including Ben More and Stob Binnein, more than 80km away to the west. Descend south on a path that runs parallel with a wall to reach a fence and stile. Don't cross the stile but turn left, following the fence down over open hillside. There is a path of sorts, but the underfoot terrain is fairly rough. Much further down the hillside the fence makes a sharp right-hand turn and continues to reach grazing land. Cross a wooden section of fence, turn left and head down the grassy slope, keeping the fence to your left. There are a couple of boggy burns to negotiate, as well as rabbitholes that could cause a nasty ankle twist.

In the base of the valley, the fence bears left. Keep right of an older fence and follow grassy vehicle tracks over a shallow burn. Stay with the old fence, but be prepared to detour right briefly to avoid boggy ground.

The fence reaches a metal gate. Bear right here to descend by an obvious track to meet the B951 beyond a small plantation. Turn left and follow the road back to the start.

Curve left here and a narrow but more obvious path zigzags up the slope, becoming clearer as height is gained.

The ascent through heather and blaeberry bushes is strenuous, but great views open out, particularly to the northeast over 16th-century Forter Castle and up Glen Isla towards the mountains of Glas Maol and Creag Leacach. The path climbs to a small cairn above Creag na Cuigeil. Walk southwest from here, the trail following a line of fenceposts across heathery hillside to dark peat hags that mark the start of the final ascent.

A mobile telephone mast dominates the summit of Mount Blair. Below this is a trig point, cairn and viewpoint indicator. Unfortunately, some of the panels are missing, but the view remains as

◀ Forter Castle from Mount Blair

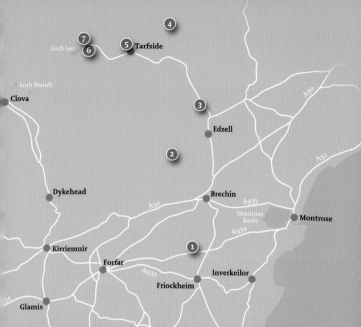

Travel north from Forfar on the A90 and the next community of any size you will encounter is Brechin. Locals proudly describe their town as a city; their church was granted cathedral status back in the 12th century. Aside from the cathedral, Brechin has become a focal point for the celebration of the county's Pictish links with the popular Pictavia Visitor Centre tracing the history of these early people whose carved stones and other artefacts are to be found all over Angus.

Evidence of prehistoric activity can be found close by at the Caterthuns, a pair of neighbouring hill forts located to the north of Brechin.

Returning to the present day, Brechin is a good starting point for adventures in Glen Esk, another of the Angus Glens. The B966 leads in via Edzell and Gannochy Bridge and a narrow, twisting route takes over from here. The hamlet of Tarfside is the only community of any size in the glen and the road ends at Invermark, an imposing shooting lodge.

From here, the track through Glen Mark is a popular approach to Scotland's most easterly Munro, Mount Keen. For less experienced walkers, there are plenty of shorter hikes over lower ground, including routes to the Rocks of Solitude, the Queen's Well and Loch Lee.

Brechin, Edzell and Glen Esk

Montreathmont Forest

Distance 6.5km Time 3 hours
Terrain flat forest tracks, quiet country
roads Map OS Explorer 389
Access no public transport

Montreathmont Forest contains native
pinewood habitats, relics of the ancient
Caledonian Forest that once carpeted
large tracts of Scotland. The trees are
home to a vast array of birds and wildlife,
including the rare capercaillie and
woodcock. Cast your eyes to the sky and
you may also spot raptors like buzzards,
kestrels and sparrowhawks.

The walk begins on the minor road that
runs northeast from Cross Roads, on the
B9113, to Brechin. It bisects
Montreathmont Forest and, 1km south of
Powsoddie, tracks branch east and west
into the trees. There is space to park at the
ends of each track, but be sure not to
block either of the gates as forest vehicles
may require access.

Walk north along the road for 200m and,
as you approach a field, turn left onto a
forest track. It runs straight ahead for a
short distance, passing through leafy
deciduous trees, before curving left.
Continue between regimented rows of
dense conifers to a junction.

Turn right and walk north to a
crossroads flanked by tall Scots pines.
These are just a small sample of the
native pines that make Montreathmont
so attractive to wildlife such as red
squirrels and red and fallow deer. Turn
left at this point to follow a pleasant
grassy track west. It soon emerges from
the more mature trees to cross a swathe
of younger saplings.

Evidence shows that Montreathmont
has been managed for forestry for more
than 150 years and it continues to be used
as a source of wood to this day. That,
however, does not deter the many birds
that make their home here. Species to look
out for include great spotted woodpecker,
green woodpecker, coal tit, blue tit, great

◀ Farmland to the north of Montreathmont Forest

tit, tree creeper and pheasant.

Further on, the track curves right and descends to meet a road beyond a metal gate. Turn left and follow the road southwest, passing Wood of Aldbar Farm, on your right, and Roadman's Cottage, on your left. Further on, as the road crosses Melgund Muir, two minor roads come in from the right. Ignore these and carry straight on until you reach the entrance to Pitkennedy Farm.

Turn left and re-enter the forest on a gravel track. The roof of a white house is visible at the top of the track, but only walk as far as a crossroads. Go left here and let a forest track lead you east.

To the south of this track, on open ground beyond the trees, an airship station was established at the end of the First World War. The RAF moored non-rigid airships here between 1918 and 1919. Few traces remain, but it

was not the only military operation within Montreathmont. In a clearing in the eastern portion of the forest, a secret listening post was built during the Second World War. An outstation of the famous Bletchley Park code-breaking centre near Milton Keynes, it continued to monitor the airwaves through the Cold War before advances in communications technology rendered it redundant in 1966. Some of the buildings remain.

The track leads through a mix of native pines and plantation conifers before eventually meeting the minor road that cuts through the forest. Turn left and follow the road back to the track ends where you started the walk.

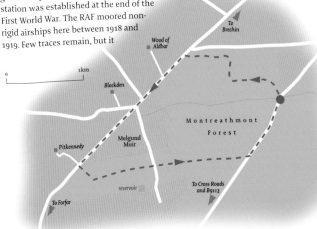

The Caterthuns

Distance 3km **Time** 1 hour **Terrain** steep
climb on good hill paths **Map** OS Explorer
389 **Access** no public transport; nearest
bus service is to Edzell, 7km away

The Caterthuns are two outstandingly
large Iron Age forts perched on prominent
hilltops at the foot of Glen Lethnot.
A narrow road bisects the pair and this
short walk links them from a car park in
the middle, which is well signed from the
hamlet of Inchbare, on the B966, 3km
south of Edzell.

It is really up to you which Caterthun
you decide to visit first. However, before
you set off, pop through the gate at the
start of the path leading to the White
Caterthun and within a small fenced
enclosure, alongside picnic tables, there is
a handy information board complete with
descriptive images of the forts. This offers

a useful insight into the layouts of the
two structures.

For the White Caterthun – so called
because of its pale ring of stones – carry
on along the path which rises steeply over
heather moor. There is a lone tree part
way up, and be sure to pause from time
to time to view the Brown Caterthun
behind you.

Approaching the fort, the path passes
an information sign and shortly thereafter
it rises over rampart ditches to reach what
remains of the drystone perimeter wall.
When it was constructed it was 12m thick
and several metres high. Now it forms an
extensive ring of rubble around the
interior of the fort. According to local
legend, a witch took just half a day to
carry the stones here in her apron. It must
have been a pretty big apron!

Despite intensive archaeological

investigations, very few artefacts have ever been found in either the White or Brown Caterthun and no one has been able to accurately date the sites. They are, however, among the best-preserved ancient hill forts in Scotland.

The path cuts across the centre of the oval enclosure, passing a deep hole, believed to have been a well or cistern where water was stored. When you reach the outer wall, you can return to the main entrance along the top of either the north or south wall. Both routes afford stunning views across the surrounding countryside.

Take the path back down to the car park and cross the road. A wooden stile marks the start of the path to the Brown Caterthun. The route follows the line of a fence across heather moor and, apart from a final sharp ascent, is fairly flat, a pleasant contrast to the short but stiff hike onto the White Caterthun.

Although similar in size, the Brown Caterthun is less clearly defined, mainly because it does not have the same ring of stone. It did, however, have four earth ramparts and various ditches.

While there is clear evidence of settlement at the White Caterthun, nothing has been uncovered to support occupation of the Brown Caterthun and there remains uncertainty over its reason for existence. Unusually for a fort, surveys suggest it had no fewer than nine entrances, making it difficult to defend.

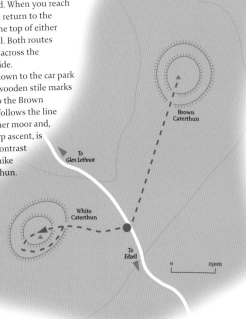

◀ View east from White Caterthun

The Blue Door and the Rocks of Solitude

Distance 5.5km **Time** 3 hours
Terrain gently undulating riverside path,
minor road; take care near steep drops
Map OS Explorer 389 **Access** bus (29A,
29C, 31, 150) from Brechin via Edzell stops
at Gannochy Bridge

North of Gannochy Bridge, a turbulent
gorge of whipping white water and inky
black pools infest the River North Esk.
Starting at an incongruous blue door set
into an old stone wall, this walk explores
the Esk's many twists and turns,
culminating in a visit to the Rocks of
Solitude, a quiet spot to sit and reflect
upon the day's watery drama.

A layby just east of Gannochy Bridge
offers limited parking at the start of the
route. Duck through the blue door in the
wall here and a woodland trail, lined with
rhododendron bushes and sheltered by
deciduous woodland, awaits the walker.
Set off along the path, but be prepared to
make the occasional detour. The first, on
the left just a few metres in, descends via
rocky steps to the Cave Pool, one of a
number of popular salmon fishing spots
on this stretch of river. To witness the
spectacle of salmon leaping as they head
upstream to spawn, the best time to visit
is October.

Continue along the main path and, just
beyond a bench, a path on the left drops
to the Salmon Pool, a ribbon of tranquil
water below a large shelf of ribbed rock.
Further on, beyond another bench, the
trail crosses a wooden bridge over a burn
and passes above the Major Pool where
the water appears bronze thanks to the
red sandstone riverbed.

Stay on the riverside path as another
parallel route comes in from the right and
follow the trail as it dips beyond a tree
stump and skirts above a steep drop to
the river on the left. Look out for red
squirrels as you go and also keep your

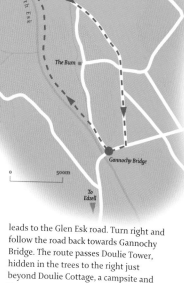

◀ Negotiating a way through the
Rocks of Solitude

pinned to a tree to the
right of the path.

The route passes the
remains of an old wire
suspension bridge and, if you
duck down onto the rocks
below this, you will find a very
narrow rocky channel pulsating
with fast-flowing water. The
trail continues to a wide junction. Bear
right here to cross a small stone
culvert and then immediately left to
rejoin the river, which is now much
more sedate. On the far bank, grassy
fields slope up towards low hills.

With rhododendron bushes lining the
path, the way becomes increasingly
narrow. Cross a bridge further on and bear
left to cross another. The path climbs for a
brief spell and, at the next junction, turn
left to enjoy a wilder and more rugged
hike above a rocky canyon. Take care, as
there is a very steep drop to your left.

Just beyond a bench in memory of Elsie
McLean on the right, a short detour out
onto a rocky promontory is highly
recommended for views up and down the
river. Overshadowed by high cliffs, the
main path continues, cutting a course
through rocks before rising towards an
information board up to the right. Below
the sign, turn left and a path descends to
the Rocks of Solitude. It is a bit of a
scramble over rough stony ground, but
well worth it.

Head back up to the sign where a path

leads to the Glen Esk road. Turn right and
follow the road back towards Gannochy
Bridge. The route passes Doulie Tower,
hidden in the trees to the right just
beyond Doulie Cottage, a campsite and
the entrance to Burn House, an 18th-
century mansion which now houses a
study and retreat centre for university
students and academics.

65

Mount Battock

Distance 15km **Time** 6 hours
Terrain tracks and hill paths with steep
climbs and boggy ground higher up;
navigation with an OS map and compass
is essential, as is hillwalking gear; dogs
should be kept on a lead across sheep
grazing land **Map** OS Explorer 395
Access limited weekday bus service (150)
from Brechin to Millden

Mount Battock is a tough wee hill. The
ascent, largely over hill tracks, is long
and arduous with some steep climbs,
while the summit is exposed to the
elements. This is a route for those with
some hillwalking experience. Aim to do
this walk on a good clear day when you
will enjoy great vistas from the summit.

Start at the telephone box just west of
Millden Lodge, where there is parking
space for a small number of cars, and set
off up the minor road to Mill of Aucheen.

Beyond the house and outbuildings, turn
right on a gravel track leading to Muir
Cottage. Bear right in front of the cottage,
head through a metal gate and continue
over grassland towards Scots pine trees.

As the track approaches the trees, it
curves left and descends to cross Hazel
Burn (either ford this or use the wooden
footbridge to the right of the track). The
track climbs away from the burn and
crosses open ground to reach a junction
1km further on.

Go right and descend to cross Burn of
Turret. Climb to a junction a few metres
up the slope, turn right and follow a track
east, rising steadily to another junction
1km up the hillside.

Turning left here, the track rises on to
Hill of Turret. It continues to climb,
steeply in places, to the summit of Hill of
Saughs. There are some fine views east
towards Clachnaben – a hill crowned with

a granite tor – which may help take your mind off the hard work.

Stay on the main track over Hill of Saughs, ignoring a track branching left, until you reach the end of the line. Where the track ends, a path continues. It descends to cross an electric fence (by a gate) and negotiates inky black peat hags in the bealach between Hill of Saughs and Mount Battock. It can be pretty wet and muddy underfoot here.

The path is not always obvious, so some careful route finding is required. However, as you climb out of the hags and cross a fence, another fence running at right angles up the slope offers a useful navigational aid (it goes all the way to the summit). The ground remains boggy until a more obvious path reveals itself further up the slope. Follow this to the top of Mount Battock. The summit boasts a trig point and there are panoramic views to reward the effort. Clachnaben can be seen to the east while Mount Keen, a Munro, is visible to the west.

Descend west, following a fence on your left down to a wooden gate. Leave the fence behind and continue west, following a faint track that leads across the col and on to Wester Cairn. Stay with the track as it curves left and descends to meet a more substantial track on the southwest slope of Wester Cairn.

Turn left and follow the track down to a metal gate. Go through the gate, stay on the track and continue to descend. It passes a row of grouse shooting butts and a wooden hut used by estate workers to reach a junction by the confluence of Black Burn and White Burn.

Go straight ahead here, the track curving round the slope of Allrey before swinging left and dropping to fenced enclosures. At a junction just prior to the enclosures, go straight on and at the next junction, by the enclosures, go left. Take the track back down to the junction above the Burn of Turret crossing and retrace your steps to Millden.

Water of Tarf

Distance 2.5km **Time** 2 hours
Terrain undulating minor road, track
Map OS Explorer 395 **Access** limited
weekday bus service (150) from Brechin
stops at Tarfside

If the weather is hot, a great way to cool
down is to go for a paddle or enjoy a wild
swim. The rivers, burns and lochs of
Angus offer numerous possibilities and
this short walk from the hamlet of
Tarfside leads to one such perfect pool on
the Water of Tarf.

Begin at the car park in the centre of
Tarfside. Join the road at the phonebox by
the car park entrance, turn left and follow
the tarmac west, crossing a bridge over
the Water of Tarf. A little further on, at a
junction, leave the main road and carry
straight on, following a sign for Milton.

This quiet single-track road passes St

Drostan's Church, a simple yet elegant
structure built in 1879. If you fancy
popping in, the door is always open.
Beyond the church, the road swings right,
passing St Drostan's Lodge, a retreat
operated by the church offering self-
catering accommodation to groups and
families. Beyond a farm shed a little
further on, the road curves left and then
right, climbing gently away from a house
on the left, passing a copse of tall Scots
pine trees, to reach a junction.

Turn right here, following a track signed
for Baillies. The way heads north through
silver birch trees, with the river down to
the right, and soon starts to descend to
cross a bridge over the Burn of Calanach.
It is not unusual to see buzzards soaring
over the moor here while oystercatchers
and curlews are more commonly spotted.

Once over the bridge, the track skirts by

the ruins of an ancient cottage and rises gently over heather moor to a three-way junction close to the cottage at Burnfoot. Go right here on a grassy track that passes a pointed slab daubed with the words 'No Fires' and 'No Camping'. It is a real pity that camping is not permitted here for it would be a fine spot for a wild pitch.

The track leads across a wide area of flat grass. Continue until there is no longer any heather to the right and then bear right towards the wooded river valley. Skirt along the top of the gorge until you reach a rough and fairly steep little path that descends to a tranquil pool between sections of faster-flowing water.

Carefully pick your way down to a small beach of sand and gravel and you will find a very decent spot for swimming or paddling. Sheltered by vertical slabs of rock and a leafy tree canopy, the gravel shelves into the water at a comfortable angle and above the pool there is a well-placed diving rock. If you don't fancy getting wet, this is a secluded spot to enjoy a picnic. To complete the walk, retrace your steps to Tarfside.

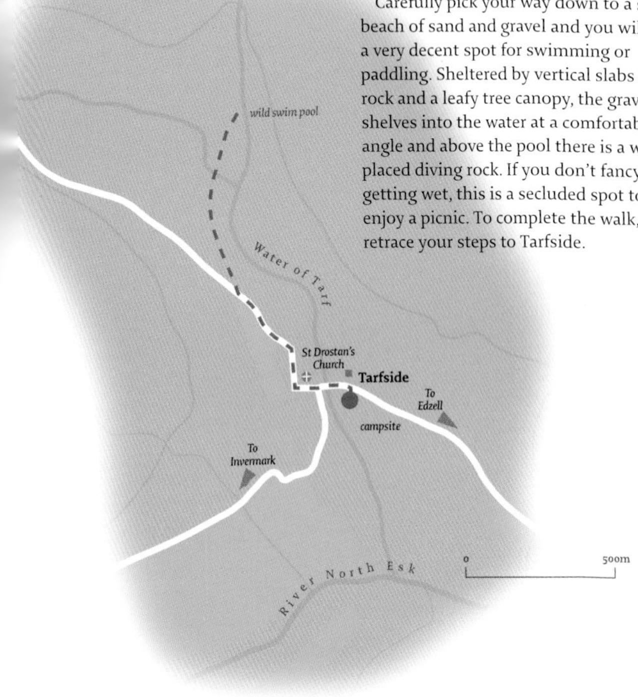

wild swim pool

Water of Tarf

St Drostan's Church

Tarfside

To Edzell

campsite

To Invermark

River North Esk

0   500m

Loch Lee

Distance 7.25km Time 3 hours
Terrain mostly flat minor road, track
Map OS Explorer 395 Access limited
weekday bus service (150) from Brechin
to Invermark

The long and winding road up Glen Esk
ends just short of Invermark Lodge, a
classic mid-Victorian shooting lodge and
once the focal point for activities on the
vast Invermark Estate. The great granite
structure overlooks Loch Lee, a reservoir
that supplies much of Angus and South
Aberdeenshire with its drinking water.

Just before the road ends, there is a
public car park. Set off from here and
follow the road west, crossing the Burn of
Branny and passing Lochlee Parish
Church, which dates from 1803 and

continues to hold occasional services.
Stay with the road, passing a track on the
right which leads into Glen Mark, and
cross the Water of Mark.

The road curves right and ends just
short of a cottage. Bear left at a postbox
and a gravel track climbs through a metal
gate to reach Invermark Castle. This solid
stone tower dates from 1526 when it was
built to guard the pass from Glen Esk to
Deeside.

Over the years the structure has been
altered and parts removed, and what
stands today is an empty shell. Sadly it is
not possible to go inside the castle for
safety reasons, but a walk around the
imposing keep is every bit as appealing as
there are plenty of interesting features to
spot, including the main entrance which,

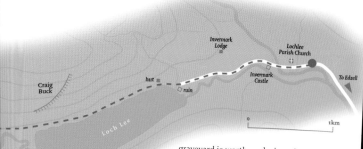

to deter attackers, sits some way above the ground. It was accessed by way of a drawbridge that opened onto the roof of a long demolished outbuilding.

Beyond the castle, the track descends and runs alongside the river, a turbulent flow of whitewater. The light, airy woodland soon thins out completely and, as the route approaches Loch Lee, Invermark Lodge and a cluster of estate buildings can be seen up to the right. To your left, the river is now more placid, sweeping arcs of water meandering through lush grassland. Ahead, however, the terrain is wilder and more rugged, steep craggy slopes descending sharply towards the loch.

Clinging to the eastern end of the loch, near Kirkton, is a ruined church and a small cemetery. St Drostan established a place of worship here in the early 7th century, although the current structure dates from the late 16th century. The

graveyard is worth exploring; there are some fascinating headstones and excellent views down the loch, but the church building itself is no more than a couple of stabilised gable walls.

Back on the track, continue west. The route passes through a gate next to a cattle grid and presses ahead down the northern shore of Loch Lee, passing below a hut. The exposed terrain means it can be very windy here, but the views towards rocky Craig Maskeldie and the Shank of Inchgrundle more than compensate for any discomfort the elements may cause. Follow the track as far as the junction near the cottage at Glenlee for great views back down Loch Lee.

Although this is the furthest point up the glen this walk explores, it is possible to go further if you have the time and energy. You can continue 5km up Glen Lee to the Stables of Lee or walk 2km up the valley and then branch left and climb to the Falls of Unich and higher Falls of Damff.

To conclude this walk, however, head back along the lochside track to the ruined church and retrace your steps from here to the car park.

◀ Graveyard at Kirkton

Glen Mark and the Queen's Well

Distance 8km **Time** 3 hours
Terrain gently undulating minor road,
tracks **Map** OS Explorer 395 **Access** limited
weekday bus service (150) from Brechin
to Invermark

In September 1861, Queen Victoria and
her husband Prince Albert passed
through Glen Mark en route from
Deeside to Glen Esk. The couple paused
briefly to take water from a spring in the
glen and to commemorate their visit an
ornate well was constructed by the Earl of
Dalhousie. It stands to this day and is the
destination for this walk.

Set off from the public car park near the
end of the Glen Esk road and follow the
road west, crossing the Burn of Branny
and passing Lochlee Parish Church. Just
before the road passes over the Water of
Mark, turn right onto a track that leads to
House of Mark, a bed and breakfast. The
route is signed for Ballater, the Queen's

Well and Mount Keen.

Below House of Mark the track forks; go
left, following a sign for the Queen's
Well, and continue through a gate a little
further on. The track rises gently through
sparse woodland before crossing open
grassland leading to heather moor. In a
short while, it passes through a metal gate
and then rises gently through the heather.

The track is well defined and easy to
follow, leading through Glen Mark to a
junction just beyond the Burn of
Glascorrie. Carry straight on here and do
likewise at a second junction, where a
track on the left drops to a bridge over the
Water of Mark.

Hemmed in by increasingly steep
hillsides, the route runs parallel with the
river, passing a large area of felled forestry
over to your left. The track follows the
course of an ancient highway called the
Mounth Road. It was originally a busy
trade route linking Glen Esk with Ballater.

◂ Sign for the Queen's Well

Rising over the western shoulder of Mount Keen, Scotland's most easterly Munro, it was by no means an easy journey, particularly in winter when snow frequently obliterated the way.

The Mounth Road is just one of a number of old highways that once crossed the hills between Deeside and Angus and Queen Victoria regularly traversed them by pony during her stays at Balmoral Castle. On September 20, 1861, she and her husband were heading for Fettercairn when they stopped for refreshment at White Well. The Glen Mark track veers away from the well but a grassy path, branching right, leads to it. Beneath stone arches, water gurgles up into a bowl that carries the inscription: 'Rest traveller, on this lonely green, and drink and pray for Scotland's Queen'.

Later in the same year, Prince Albert died, but Queen Victoria visited Glen Mark again in 1865 with her daughter Princess Helena. They lunched at Glenmark House, an isolated cottage just north of the well, before taking the water.

From the Queen's Well, it is possible to continue up the Mounth Road and make an ascent of Mount Keen or bear west to visit waterfalls and search out Balnamoon's Cave, hiding place of James Carnegie, a Jacobite who sought refuge from government troops in the upper reaches of Glen Mark following the Battle of Culloden in 1746. Local people brought him food and warned him when Redcoats were in the area, and he managed to successfully evade capture until he was eventually pardoned. The cave is well hidden amongst rocks and not easy to find. To complete this walk, retrace your steps down Glen Mark.

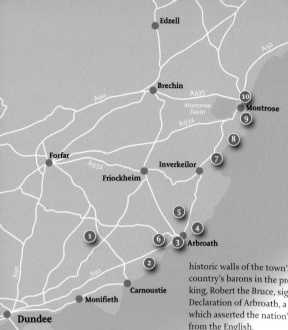

The Angus coast stretches north from the Firth of Tay to the mouth of the River North Esk. It encompasses great swathes of golden sand, dramatic cliffs, rocky coves and a proud maritime heritage. From the earliest times, ports like Arbroath and Montrose pioneered seafaring trade routes with the Continent and developed thriving fishing industries while smaller fleets operated out of harbours like East Haven, Auchmithie and Usan.

Arbroath holds a special place in Scottish history. For it was within the historic walls of the town's abbey that the country's barons in the presence of their king, Robert the Bruce, signed the Declaration of Arbroath, a document which asserted the nation's independence from the English.

While the county's fishing industry has declined dramatically, Arbroath Harbour is now a busy marina and pleasurecraft base and the port of Montrose handles significant commercial traffic, much of it connected to the offshore oil industry.

Improved wastewater treatment along the coast has seen a significant rise in the cleanliness of bathing waters, an increase in bird life and regular visits by dolphins and porpoises.

A coastal trail is slowly being developed, but in the meantime there are plenty of bracing seafront strolls to enjoy and a range of easy walks that head inland from the sea.

The Deil's Heid near Arbroath

Along the Angus Coast

Crombie Loch

Distance 5km **Time** 2 hours **Terrain** flat
lochside path, track **Map** OS Explorer 382
Access no public transport

Crombie Loch was created in 1866 to
provide water for the growing population
and expanding industries of Dundee.
Today the reservoir sits at the heart of a
country park with a network of walking
trails. This route follows the Discovery
Trail around the loch.

Set off from the information hut in the
main car park (a parking charge is levied)
and follow the signed Birch Wood Trail.
Carry straight on at the first junction you
encounter and the path runs above leafy
Crombie Den to the dam at the eastern
end of Crombie Loch.

During the early 19th century, Dundee's
demand for water was insatiable. In 1854 a
reservoir was completed at Monikie, but it
soon became clear this alone would not
slake the city's thirst. Crombie

Den and an adjacent quarry were
soon identified as the location for a
second reservoir.

Crombie no longer has any input into
the public water supply. It was last used
to supply water to Carnoustie in 1981 and
two years later Crombie Country Park,
which covers 102 hectares of land, was
officially opened.

When you reach the dam, turn right,
following a Discovery Trail sign (the route
has yellow waymarker posts), and cross a
green metal bridge spanning the reservoir
outflow. Continue across the dam towards
a wooden jetty used by anglers. Above the
jetty, the path curves left, entering trees.
Tall pines dominate here, but as
the route progresses it
passes through

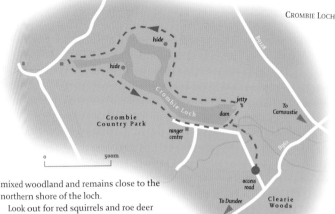

mixed woodland and remains close to the northern shore of the loch.

Look out for red squirrels and roe deer lurking among the trees and in the canopy above you may spot coal tits, goldcrests, crossbills and woodpeckers.

The path surface is excellent (kids will be able to take their bikes around the loch) and at points along the way short detours can be made to the edge of the water. There are also various points of interest, signed with a yellow thistle logo.

Beyond the first of these, which offers an insight into the life of a tree, the path swings right to reach a junction, just over a wooden footbridge. Go left here and, a little further on, the path curves right. At the next junction, turn left and a narrow path winds through the trees to an elevated hide with information on the park's roe deer population.

Continue along the path and, at the next junction, go left. The trail continues through the trees for a way before crossing grassland where wildflowers attract butterflies in the summer.

As the western tip of the loch is approached, the water becomes

increasingly reedy and it is here that you may spot grebes, assorted ducks and a variety of other waterfowl.

At the end of the reservoir, the route crosses a wooden bridge and swings right to reach a gate and stile. Don't cross but instead bear left to enter a clearing where, adjacent to an old cottage, there is an outdoor display of traditional farming implements.

Turn left for the Discovery Trail and the path heads along the southern shore of the reservoir. Along the way, look out for a signed detour on the left that leads to a hide that contains lots of information on Crombie's feathered inhabitants and seasonal visitors.

In due course, the main trail meets a surfaced road and, a few metres on, a concrete ramp leads up onto a grassy embankment above the water. Follow this past the park ranger centre to the dam and then retrace your steps along the Birch Wood Trail to the car park.

◀ Boats at the anglers' jetty

East Haven Beach

Distance 5.5km **Time** 2 hours 30
Terrain sand and shingle beach, flat
coastal path **Map** OS Explorer 382
Access bus (40E, 73A) from Dundee stops
in East Haven

Established around a natural harbour in
1214, East Haven is one of Scotland's
oldest fishing villages. In its heyday, it
boasted a thriving fleet of boats, as well
as an inn, bakery and brewery. Much has
changed over the years (the inn, bakery
and brewery are long gone), but the
fishing industry remains, albeit on a very
small scale.

From the centre of the village, pass
beneath the railway line to reach a public
car park and public toilets above the
harbour. Leave the car park and go left
along a surfaced track. When you reach a
small boatyard on your left, turn right and
follow a grassy path down to the beach.

The crescent of golden sand has long
been popular with bathers and the Queen

and her sister, the late Princess Margaret,
frequently picnicked here during
childhood holidays at Glamis Castle.

Turn left and walk along the beach,
crossing the outflow of a small burn. The
terrain is a mix of sand, shingle and rock,
and the salty pools left by the receding
tide attract birds like oystercatchers, gulls
and guillemots.

Some 2km from East Haven, the route
rounds a headland – and sandstone cliffs
to the north of Arbroath can be seen on
the horizon. In time, the town itself
comes into view and as the beach curves
left it passes below a line of concrete
blocks on top of the dunes to your left.
These anti-tank blocks were constructed
during the Second World War as part of
Britain's coastal defences, and there were
also at least four pillboxes built here.

Continue along the beach until you
reach a strip of rock armour, more recent
coastal defences aimed at combating
erosion. Part way along, there is a

◀ Wartime defences in the dunes

concrete-clad outflow pipe. Leave the beach here and climb onto a large grassy bank. A few metres inland, you will meet a grassy path. Join this and turn left.

This grassy bank has not always been so green. It was for decades the site of a factory producing bitumen. Known locally as Dowrie Works, the North British Chemical Works was established towards the end of the 19th century and continued in operation until 1970 when it was closed down and demolished.

The path runs straight for a short distance before curving right, dropping to a wide gap in a post and wire fence. Go through this and continue along the path as it crosses grassland between sand dunes to your left and a railway line to the right. The route runs southwest, passing below a large wastewater treatment plant built on the site of a wartime airfield at Hatton. Here, the strip of grassland between the coastline and railway narrows and the path is drawn towards the railway, running alongside the tracks for a way.

Pass a concrete hut on the opposite side of the railway and a little further on the path reaches a gap in a fence and a signpost. Go through the gap and carry straight on. The path runs a narrow course between the railway and beach before passing through two grassy fields where wildflowers attract butterflies and bees.

At the end of the second field, the path crosses a wooden footbridge with rope handrails. Once over, turn right and a path, initially sandy, leads back to the car park.

waterworks

North Sea

0   500m

ath
**East
Haven**

To Carnoustie

Arbroath seafront

Distance 5km **Time** 2 hours **Terrain** flat
seafront esplanade, pavement, paths
Map OS Explorer 382 **Access** Arbroath is
well served by buses from Dundee and
other towns in Angus, and has a railway
station on the East Coast Main Line

Arbroath Harbour was established in the
12th century and in its heyday it boasted a
thriving fishing industry. Over the years
the fleet of boats has rapidly declined, but
the famous Arbroath Smokie – a smoked
haddock delicacy – continues to be
produced using traditional methods in
backyard smokehouses on the quayside.

Located on the quayside, Arbroath
Harbour Visitor Centre celebrates the
town's maritime heritage and is an
excellent starting point for this walk, with
plenty of parking close at hand. Head

through a half-arch in the blue wall at the
right-hand end of the front of the
building, turn left and a paved footpath
leads to the neighbouring Signal Tower
Museum. Admission is free and the
museum, which has a fascinating display
on the construction of the Bell Rock
Lighthouse, is open all year.

Beyond the museum entrance, turn left
and follow a footpath down the south
side of the building towards the sea. The
route curves right and heads along an
esplanade, passing Gayfield Park, home of
Arbroath Football Club.

Further along the front, a road comes in
from the right. Continue straight ahead,
now walking on a pavement running
alongside the road to the West Links
Recreation Area. Where the road curves
right, go left on a surfaced path that runs
between the sea on your left and a
paddling pool to your right. There's an ice
cream hut on the other side of the pool if
you fancy a cone.

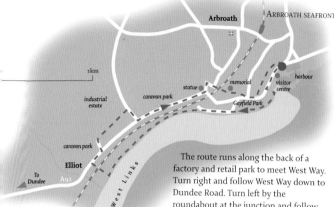

The route crosses a ramp running down to the sandy West Links beach and continues past a children's play area, on the right. A little further on is Kerr's Miniature Railway, a popular seafront distraction that has been thrilling children and adults alike since 1935.

At the end of the esplanade, a gravel path continues over parkland. Carry on along this seafront trail until you reach a sign, pointing right, for Elliot. Turn right, leaving the path at the sign, and head over grass to a metal footbridge spanning a railway line. Cross and, on the other side, walk straight on to a pedestrian crossing on Dundee Road (A92).

Cross the road, walk to the left of a landscape area and then turn right, following the pavement alongside Dundee Road. Go past the entrance to Elliot Caravan Park and, at the next road junction, turn left, following a sign for Hospitalfield. At the top of the road, turn right, following a path, again signed for Hospitalfield.

The route runs along the back of a factory and retail park to meet West Way. Turn right and follow West Way down to Dundee Road. Turn left by the roundabout at the junction and follow the pavement, heading into Arbroath. Pass the Red Lion Caravan Park and a Territorial Army base, both on your left, and continue to the next road junction. On parkland to your left, there is a statue celebrating the signing of the famous Declaration of Arbroath – a treaty for Scottish independence – at the town's abbey in 1320.

Turn left, head up the road to a crossing point, cross and follow a surfaced path up to a bridge over the railway line. Once over, follow another path to the town's war memorial. Descend from here to Tuttie's Neuk Inn.

A pavement runs along the front of the inn and past houses to a road junction. Cross the road coming in from the left and follow a paved path running parallel to Dundee Road. It skirts to the right of low-rise blocks of flats and then passes The Bell Rock fish and chip shop. Continue on the footway to a pedestrian crossing, on the other side of which is Arbroath Harbour Visitor Centre.

◄ Arbroath Harbour smokehouse

Seaton Cliffs and the Forbidden Cave

Distance 5.5km Time 2 hours 30
Terrain good coastal path with some short
but steep climbs; take care as it runs along
the top of unguarded sea cliffs
Map OS Explorer 382 Access Arbroath is
well served by buses from Dundee and
other towns in Angus, and has a railway
station on the East Coast Main Line

**Rising to the north of Arbroath, Seaton
Cliffs offer one of the most spectacular
walks in Angus. Along the coastal trail
there are high cliffs, sandstone arches,
deep inlets, secret coves, a sea stack and
caves to explore.**

The walk starts at the east end of
Victoria Park, next to the public toilets at
Whiting Ness. A tarmac path leaves the
park at an information board and climbs
steeply to a junction. Go straight on,
following a sign for Seaton Cliffs.

Passing through the Seaton Cliffs
Nature Reserve – where black-headed
gulls, shags and guillemots may be

spotted on the rocks – the route rises
steadily to the Needle's E'e (Needle's Eye),
a narrow hole worn into the soft
sandstone by the sea. A fairly steep path
on the right leads down to this
interesting geological feature and there
are some cracking views up and down the
coast. Look out, too, for dolphin – you
may see them swimming offshore.

The main path continues along the top
of a deep rocky cove and, beyond this,
grassy trails branch right to various
viewpoints. Much time can be spent
exploring the clifftops and there is plenty
to see below, including deep chasms,
rocky caves and narrow inlets. But do take
great care; there are perilously steep drops.

The route curves inland at Dickmont's
Den, a deep channel cutting into the
coastline. Look out for a cave on the
northern side of the inlet as you follow
the path round the top of the channel and
back towards the sea.

Another geological treat lies just

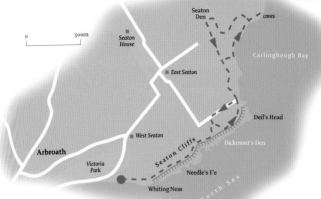

0   500m

Seaton
Den

caves

Seaton
House

Carlingheugh Bay

East Seaton

Deil's Head

West Seaton

Dickmont's Den

Seaton Cliffs

Arbroath

Victoria
Park

Needle's E'e

Whiting Ness

North Sea

round the next corner – the Deil's Heid (Devil's Head), a stack with a wonderfully evil face that glares out to sea. There's a good viewpoint just before the stack is reached and, depending on the state of the tide, it is possible to venture down over slabs of sandstone to its base.

Beyond the Deil's Heid, the path curves left to reach a junction, a track on the left leading into fields. Carry straight on along the coastal path here to reach the wide Carlingheugh Bay with a sliver of white sand breaking up the rocky foreshore.

The path swings right, passing above two shingle bays, and just beyond a post on the left carrying the mark 'AS21', a grassy path on the right descends to the beach. To the right, there's a sandstone arch. Head north round the bay – walking either on the beach or a grassy path above the sand – to the next headland. There are two caves here, both accessible when the tide is out. The first is not very deep but the second – the Forbidden Cave – tunnels through the headland, emerging into a concealed bay beyond. Headroom is low within the cave and a torch is essential. Keep an eye on the tide to ensure you do not get cut off.

At the north end of Carlingheugh Bay, a gravel path and steps rise to meet the coastal path. Turn left and follow the path into Seaton Den. As it enters the wooded valley, the path splits (there's a marker with 'AS27' on it at this junction). Go left and descend to a signpost. Following an arrow for Arbroath, go left and cross a small burn. The path climbs and, at the top of the slope, heads back towards the coast, skirting alongside fields.

Continue until you reach the junction between the Deil's Heid and Carlingheugh Bay encountered earlier in the walk. Go right and follow the track up through a field. Go left at the next junction and the route leads to Dickmont's Den. Retrace your steps from here along the coastal path to Whiting Ness.

◀ Coastal cliffs at Seaton

St Vigeans and the Picts

Distance 8km **Time** 3 hours
Terrain mostly flat paths and minor
roads **Map** OS Explorer 382 **Access** bus
(43) from Arbroath Bus Station stops at
Kirkton, 1km from St Vigeans

The red sandstone church at St Vigeans,
on the northern edge of Arbroath, is one
of the most picturesque kirks in
Scotland. Sitting atop a prominent
mound, it overlooks a crescent of lovely
cottages, one of which houses a museum
of ancient carved Pictish stones.

The walk starts at a small car park across
the Brothock Water from the church (it is
well signed from the A92 Arbroath to
Montrose road). Leave the car park by its
main entrance and turn left, following a
sign for St Vigeans Pictish Stones. Cross a
bridge over the Brothock Water and turn
right, walking along a narrow lane below
the church.

Turn right beyond an area of grass with a
park bench to enter a small cemetery. The
way runs through a grove of neatly clipped
yew trees to reach a wooden footbridge
over the burn on the right. Cross and turn
left, joining a former railway trackbed.

The path follows the trackbed, running
north alongside the Brothock Water.
Around 1km further on, it crosses a road
next to a restored mill.

The way continues northwards, passing
the entrance to a house after 500m. Beyond
this point, the path skirts behind a row of
houses before passing through a cutting
and under an old railway bridge. At the end
of the cutting, you can see, on your right,
Letham Grange, a former Victorian
mansion now run as a hotel with two golf
courses. The path arrives at the remains of
the former Colliston Station.

Built by the Caledonian Railway, it
opened in 1839 to serve the nearby village
of Colliston and closed to passengers in
1955. A few metres on, the old railway

◀ Kirkside Cottages, St Vigeans

trackbed meets a road. Turn left and follow the road up through a deep cutting. Ignore the entrance to East Mains of Colliston Farm on the right, and turn left at the next road junction.

A quiet country road, lined with leafy deciduous trees, heads south, descending briefly before curving up between fields. Carry straight on at the next junction to reach Peebles Farm. On from here are the remains of a wartime airfield, old hangers now used to store farm machinery

and straw. This was once connected to the RM Condor marine base, which was a naval aerodrome during the Second World War.

Continue south, ignoring a track on the left, and the road runs between fields before passing the high perimeter fence of RM Condor to reach a junction at Mains of Letham farm. Carry straight on here, passing a pair of cottages on the left, and continue through the farm.

The road curves left and then right before running straight towards the northern outskirts of Arbroath. At the next junction, where St Vigeans Manse – a modern bungalow – sits on the right, a section of disused tarmac on the left offers a shortcut to a minor road that descends steeply to St Vigeans.

Once in the village, explore the church and its graveyard – where there are some fascinating old headstones – before heading along the crescent of old sandstone cottages to St Vigeans Museum of Carved Stones, which is open all year. Follow the crescent round to the bridge over the Brothock Water and cross to return to the car park.

Passage to Arbirlot

Distance 5km **Time** 2 hours
Terrain undulating paths, tracks, quiet
country roads; keep dogs on a lead across
cattle grazing land **Map** OS Explorer 382
Access bus (39, 73) from Dundee to
Arbroath stops at Elliot

The trackbed of the former Carmyllie Light
Railway, built in the 19th century to
transport quarried stone, provides a well-
graded path for this easy hike from Elliot,
on the southern edge of Arbroath, through
Kelly Den to the pretty village of Arbirlot.

Start at Elliot car park, accessed from the
roundabout by the golf course on the
southern approach to Arbroath. Head
north out of the car park, crossing the
access road and, to the right of Elliot
Bridge, go through a metal gate, following
a sign for Arbirlot.

A grassy path leads into mixed
woodland, shadowing the Elliot Water
upstream to reach a metal gate. Go
through this to follow the path across an
open field where cattle frequently graze.

The old railway line originally ran from
a junction with the mainline at Elliot to
quarries operated by Lord Panmure at
Carmyllie. In 1854, he built the railway to
ferry his stone to market. Initially horse-
drawn, steam locomotives were later
introduced and in 1900 the first passenger
services began. Thanks to some severe
gradients, travellers enjoyed a slow but
scenic journey.

At the far end of the first field, the path
goes through a gate leading into a second
field. Continue along the grassy path,
passing a green pond in a leafy hollow on
the right, to the far end of the field where
there is another gate, leading on to a
track. Follow the track for 50m to reach a
gate on the left. Go through the gate,
following a sign for Arbirlot, and descend
to a wooden footbridge over a small burn.

On the other side of the bridge, steps
take you up to a path which runs between
woodland on your left – the private

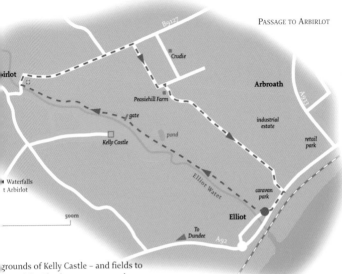

grounds of Kelly Castle – and fields to your right. The four-storey towerhouse dates from the 16th century and was restored in 1870. In a while, the trail drops down to accompany the Elliot Water.

As you near Arbirlot, the path passes below a small water treatment plant, beyond which you climb a set of steps. Look upstream here to see small waterfalls on the Elliot Water beneath a stone roadbridge. The route passes above the waterfalls and runs alongside a wall on the right – above which is a cemetery – to reach stone steps.

Climb the steps to reach Arbirlot. Turn right and follow the pavement as it runs alongside the wall of Arbirlot Parish Church. At the next junction, go right. The pavement continues along the church wall before heading out of the village.

When the pavement ends, continue on the road, which climbs steadily before flattening off at speed limit signs.

At the next road junction, carry straight on along the B9127 for 200m to reach a track on the right leading to Peasiehill Farm (the 'Private Road' sign here is aimed at vehicular traffic rather than pedestrians). Go right, following a sign for Elliot and take the gravel track south towards the farm. As you approach sheds, the track curves left and then right and, at the far end of the farmyard, it swings left again, descending between fields to reach a vast maltings complex.

Here the route curves right, passing alongside the maltings and other industrial buildings to reach a metal gate. Below this point a surfaced road runs between a caravan park and factory to meet the A92. Turn right and follow the pavement to Elliot car park.

Lunan Bay and Red Castle

Distance 10km **Time** 3 hours 30
Terrain Mainly flat with some short
climbs; minor road, sandy beach, clifftop
path **Map** OS Explorer 382 **Access** bus
(30, 39) from Arbroath to Montrose stops
at Inverkeilor, 4km from Lunan

A stunning swathe of golden sand,
Lunan Bay stretches between steep,
craggy headlands. Perched above the
dunes is the striking ruin of Red Castle
and, at the southern end of the bay, there
is a pair of tiny hamlets seemingly
forgotten by the passage of time.

The walk begins at Lunan Bay car park.
Head out of the car park and follow the
access track back up to the hamlet of
Lunan, passing through Seahorse Stables.
When you reach the road, turn left and
follow it south, passing the entrance to
Lunan House Nursing Home and then a
church and graveyard. The road crosses
the Lunan Water by an old stone bridge

and continues through an avenue of tall
trees. Keep your eyes peeled for a path on
the left that climbs steeply, passing
through a metal gate, to Red Castle.

Perched atop a promontory, the red
sandstone castle was established in the
12th century as a hunting seat by William
the Lion. Now ruined and in imminent
danger of collapse, it consists of a 13th-
century fragment of wall and the rather
precarious remains of a 15th-century
tower. It is a fine viewpoint from which to
cast your eyes over Lunan Bay and the
rolling breakers of the North Sea.

The path runs between these two main
portions of the castle before descending
steeply (stay to the left of the cottages
below) to the beach. Wander along the
south bank of the Lunan Water towards
the sea, passing through a line of old
concrete blocks, then bear right and
follow the beach south.

A wide expanse of white sand extends

towards the headland at Ethie Haven, 2km away. The walking is easiest if you stick to the hard sand near the edge of the water. The large nets pegged out at intervals along the beach are used to catch salmon, luring the unsuspecting fish in and trapping them when the sea recedes.

At the southern end of the bay is Corbie Knowe, a haphazard settlement of rustic beach huts, cabins and caravans. Head up the beach to a small parking area, and between two large concrete blocks on the left a narrow gravel path, signed for Ethie, leads to a wooden footbridge spanning a burn. Cross, bear right and a path rises behind the huts to the top of the cliffs, skirting above the south end of the bay to reach a more substantial farm track.

Carry straight on here to Ethie Haven, a hamlet of old stone cottages built originally to house fishermen and their families. Time has passed this place by – to the extent that mains electricity only reached the community in recent years.

You can make your way a little further along the coast by following a grassy path below a line of wooden huts to a couple of tiny pebble beaches sheltered under the headland beyond. Here the route ends and the best way back is to retrace your steps along the clifftop track and path to Corbie Knowe.

Walk north along Lunan Bay to Red Castle and, at low water, it is possible to paddle across the mouth of the Lunan Water, thereby cutting out the climb up to Red Castle and the trek along the road back to the car park. This also gives you an opportunity to explore the northern portion of the beach. A well-walked path leads up through the dunes to the car park.

Boddin Point

Distance 3km **Time** 1 hour 30
Terrain undulating coastal path, quiet
country road **Map** OS Explorer 382
Access bus (39, 47) from Montrose to
Ferryden, 4km from the start

Jutting into the North Sea, Boddin Point
is dominated by its historic limekilns.
This 18th-century complex was part
of a thriving industry that, together
with farming and fishing, supported
families on the remoter coastal margins
of the county.

The walk begins at a small parking area
opposite the start of a track leading into
Boddin Farm. Set off down the minor
road, passing a cottage on the right, to
reach Boddin Salmon Station, now a
house. To the right of the house, a grassy
track descends to Boddin Point.

Vast limekilns dominate the
promontory. Built in 1750 by Robert Scott
of nearby Dunninald Castle, the stone
kilns processed lime that was then
shipped out by sea. On the west side of
the point are the remains of an old
harbour and slipway, close to where a trio
of abandoned wooden fishing boats now
lie rotting.

Take care when exploring the kilns;
thanks to their antiquity and ongoing
coastal erosion they are dangerously
derelict. The view from the top, however,
is excellent, but don't venture too near
the edge.

Once you have finished exploring the
point, head back up the track to Boddin
Salmon Station and turn right, following
a grassy path signed for Boddin Bothy.
Processing lime was not the only industry

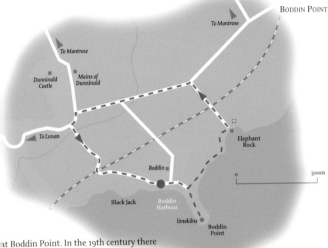

at Boddin Point. In the 19th century there was a thriving salmon fishing industry here, complete with harbour, icehouse and accommodation for fishermen.

Don't descend to the bothy – a simple white cottage sitting adjacent to a line of derelict fishermen's houses – but continue on the main path which runs alongside a field boundary wall.

Further on, the path curves left and rises above Elephant Rock. The inspiration for the name is obvious – thanks to a pair of natural arches, the great bluff of rock resembles an elephant, its trunk dipping into the sea.

The path ends at a tiny clifftop cemetery where an unusual headstone can be found. The grave of George Ramsay indicates that he was born in 1859 but died in 1840, 19 years earlier. Clearly it was an error in the inscription that no one ever decided to rectify.

A more tragic tale of infant and youthful mortality is to be found close by on a tombstone erected by local farmer Peter Keill who lost four of his children in the 1830s and 1840s.

Leave the cemetery and head north on a grassy track. The route passes beneath a railway line and rises gently between fields to meet a minor road at a metal gate. Turn left and follow the road west. There are fine sea views south and, to the northeast, it is possible to make out Scurdie Ness Lighthouse and Montrose Bay beyond.

The route passes Dunninald Mains Farm, across fields to the right, to reach a road junction. Turn left here and, at the next junction, go left, following a sign for Boddin. The road descends through farmland, crossing the railway once again to reach the parking area below Boddin Farm.

◄ Old boat at Boddin Point

91

Scurdie Ness Lighthouse

Distance 3.5km **Time** 2 hours
Terrain mostly flat village streets and
surfaced path **Map** OS Explorer 382
Access bus (39, 47) from Montrose to
Ferryden

Scurdie Ness Lighthouse has been
protecting coastal shipping and safely
guiding boats into the Port of Montrose
for more than 140 years. Occupying a
prominent headland at the southern end
of Montrose Bay, it is the destination for
this bracing estuary walk.

Start at William Street car park in
Ferryden. Walk east on William Street and
continue along King Street until you
reach a lane on the right leading into
Victoria Square. Head up this lane and,
ignoring Victoria Square on your left,
continue straight ahead, rising to a brown
wooden hut. Below the hut, go left on a
path, following a sign for the lighthouse.

The path climbs to meet a
road. Turn left and continue to
the end of the road. A
surfaced path leads on from
here, running above the
estuary of the River South
Esk. Along the stony
shoreline, keep your eyes
peeled for gulls, oystercatchers
and razorbills and you may also see
bottlenose dolphins swimming offshore.

The route passes a seating area and, a
little further on, two concrete pillboxes
lurk in the undergrowth to the left of the
path. These were built to protect the
estuary during the Second World War and

Rossie
Island

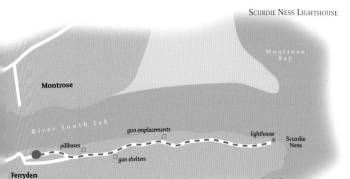

Montrose Bay

Montrose

River South Esk

gun emplacements

pillboxes

lighthouse

Scurdie Ness

gun shelters

Ferryden

To Lunan

0   500m

...are among a number of defensive structures on the coast here.

A little further on, you pass two brick-built gun shelters in a field on the right. These were manned by the Home Guard and formed part of the Montrose harbour defences. Where the track curves right, accompanied by a metal barrier, there are two gun emplacements in the slope below. To reach these, you must leave the track at the start of the barrier and scramble down through the undergrowth.

The first has a fairly large concrete frontage, complete with a plaque inscribed by its Polish builders. Sadly, a metal grill across the opening prevents further exploration and you must content yourself with the briefest of glimpses of this subterranean bunker. The second, further round the slope, is small, heavily overgrown and only just visible.

Back on the track, walk round the top of the slope to reach a white conical stone tower. This is one of two navigational aids (the other is below the lighthouse) designed to assist ships negotiating the estuary. Known as the East and West Beacons they date from the 18th century and were constructed from rubble and mortar. East Beacon is the taller of the pair.

At the end of the track is the lighthouse. Built by David and Thomas Stevenson, it was first lit on 1 March, 1870. The white tower is 39m high and there are 170 steps climbing from the base to the light. Although the light continues to operate, Scurdie Ness was automated in 1987 and is no longer manned. The former keepers' cottages now form a private dwelling. During the Second World War, the lighthouse was temporarily painted black to prevent enemy shipping or aircraft spotting it at night.

On reaching the lighthouse, you may wish to proceed further round the coast. Sandy Braes, a pleasant beach, is 500m further on along a signed coastal path while the rocks around Scurdie Ness are a good place to spot cormorants and guillemots. When you have finished exploring the area, return to Ferryden by the same route.

Montrose Bay

Distance 9.25km **Time** 4 hours
Terrain sandy beach, level paths
Map OS Explorer 382 **Access** Montrose is
well served by buses from Dundee and
towns in Angus, and has a railway station
on the East Coast Main Line

**Tramp the glorious golden sands of
Montrose Bay and then venture inland
over Charleton & Kinnaber Links to visit
the remains of an old airfield, complete
with bunkers to explore.**

Begin at Montrose Seafront Splash
where there is plenty of parking, a café and
other seasonal attractions. Opposite Traill
Pavilion, descend a flight of steps to the
beach. If the tide is high, the base of the
steps can be submerged. If this is the case, a
gap in the dunes just north of the pavilion
leads to a wooden ramp onto the sand.

Head north along the beach, following
the line of the dunes below Links of
Montrose. The bay has suffered at the
hands of coastal erosion and, along the
way, there are various points where rock

armour has been constructed in a bid to
break the powerful waves and protect the
delicate dune systems which provide a
habitat for birds and other wildlife.

The beach walk continues for 4km,
heading towards the estuary of the River
North Esk and the northern boundary of
Angus. About 1.5km before the estuary is
reached, the dunes reduce in height,
forming a rolling series of low mounds.
Look out for an obvious gap in the dunes
where a path runs inland to a derelict
cottage. Salmon fishermen formerly used
this, and the poles adjacent to the bothy
were where they hung their nets out to dry.

At the front of the cottage a grassy path
leads back towards the dunes, passing
between the poles on your left and a
conifer plantation to the right. The path
curves right and runs south between the
dunes and the woodland. Ignoring
periodic tracks going into the trees on
your right, continue to the south end of
the plantation.

Turn right and a path runs along the edge
[of] the trees to meet a track. On the left there is
[a] metal pedestrian gate. Go through this and,
[ke]eping a fence to your left, walk south on a
[pa]th crossing heathland. You are now within
[th]e former Montrose Airfield.

The Royal Flying Corps established Britain's
[fir]st operational military airfield here in 1912.
[It] played a vital role in both the First and
[Se]cond World Wars and in peacetime was
[us]ed occasionally by light aircraft, by
[Br]itish Airways helicopters for night
[tr]aining and by RAF Hercules aircraft.

The airfield is no longer operational,
[al]though parts of the runway and
[so]me of the hangars remain. As you
[w]alk, you will pass a series of
[co]ncrete bunkers constructed
[ar]ound the perimeter.

The path passes alongside a
[go]lf course before curving right
[to] reach a metal gate next to
[B]roomfield Golf Driving Range.
[B]eyond the gate, follow a wide
[co]ncrete road, formerly an
[ai]rfield taxiway, towards
[M]ontrose. This curves right to
[r]each a small football stadium
[a]nd bike track.

At the end of the bike track, turn left on a
[r]oad and, just before you reach a recycling
[c]entre, go left through a metal pedestrian
[g]ate. A narrow trail skirts along the edge of
[t]he golf course, leading to a surfaced path.
[T]urn left and follow this past Curlie Pond
[t]o meet Dorward Road.

Cross Dorward Road, turn left and
follow the pavement past the
clubhouses of Montrose Caledonia Golf
Club and Royal Montrose Golf Club. Go
straight on and the road leads back to
the Traill Pavilion.

Index